THE RANDOM HOUSE BOOK OF 1001 WONDERS OF SCIENCE

Brian and Brenda Williams

Random House 🏠 New York

CONTENTS

Atoms 4

The Elements 14

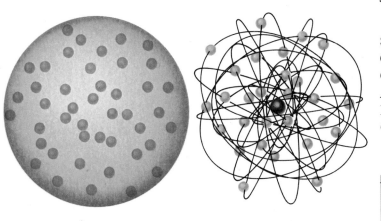

Electricity 30

First American edition, 1990

Copyright © 1989 by Grisewood & Dempsey Ltd. All rights reserved under International and Pan-American Copyright Conventions. Published in the United States by Random House, Inc., New York. Originally published in Great Britain by Kingfisher Books Limited, a Grisewood & Dempsey Company, in 1989.

LIBRARY OF CONGRESS CATALOGING-IN-PUBLICATION DATA:
Williams, Brian.
  The Random House Book of 1001 wonders of science / by Brian and Brenda Williams.
    p.   cm.
  Includes index.
  SUMMARY: Questions and answers explore such areas of science as electricity, light, space, and the elements.
  ISBN: 0-679-80080-8 (trade); 0-679-90080-2 (lib. bdg.)
    1. Science—Miscellanea—Juvenile literature. [1. Science—Miscellanea. 2. Questions and answers] I. Williams, Brenda. II. Title. III. Title: Random House book of one thousand and one wonders of science.
  Q163.W514   1990   500—dc20   89-3954

Manufactured in Italy   1 2 3 4 5 6 7 8 9 0

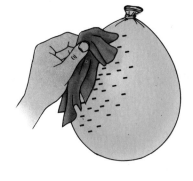
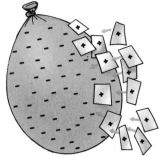

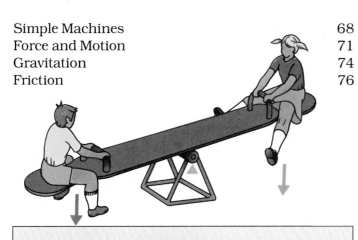

ATOMS

What is an atom?

An atom is the smallest unit of a chemical element – iron or copper, for example – to have its own recognizable identity. Scientists can tell the atoms of one element from those of another by their structure. Atoms are the building blocks of the elements which make up all matter in the universe.

What does the word *atom* mean?

The word *atom* comes from the Greek word *atomos*, meaning "uncuttable." The scientists of ancient Greece thought that an atom was the smallest thing that existed: it could not be divided. Modern scientists, by splitting the atom, showed that this is not so. But the atom is the smallest unit that behaves as a stable chemical element.

If an atom was as big as your fingernail, your hand would be huge.

How big is an atom?

Atoms measure less than one ten-millionth of an inch across. So a page of this book is about two million atoms thick! If an atom were the size of your fingernail, your hand would be large enough to pick up the Earth.

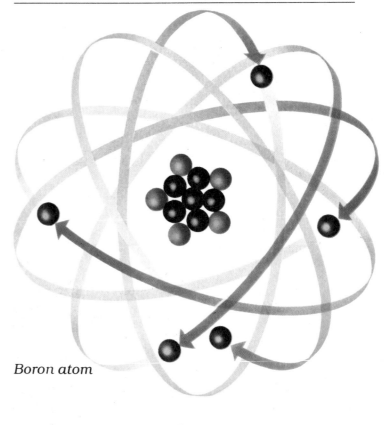

Boron atom

How is a tiny atom like the entire solar system?

Atoms are made up of tiny particles moving around a center called the nucleus. This is a lot like the way in which planets in our solar system orbit the Sun.

Can you see an atom?

Atoms are too small to be seen with the naked eye. But scientists using high-powered electron microscopes have photographed atoms. They look like fuzzy white dots.

Is anything smaller than an atom?

Yes. The nucleus at the center of an atom is ten thousand times smaller than the atom itself. Electrons, which orbit the nucleus, are smaller still.

Electrons orbit the nucleus as the planets orbit the Sun.

Is there anyplace in the Universe where no atoms are found?

As far as we know, there are atoms everywhere in the Universe, even in the near-vacuum of space.

Atoms exist in all parts of the Universe.

How many different kinds of atom are there?

There are 92 different chemical elements found in nature. Therefore there are 92 different kinds of atoms forming these separate elements. A few other elements and atoms have been made by scientists in the laboratory.

What is an atom made of?

At the center of an atom is its nucleus, which is made up of tiny particles called protons and neutrons. Orbiting the nucleus are other particles called electrons, held in place by electrical charges. The arrangement of protons, neutrons, and electrons is different for each kind of atom.

How big is the nucleus of an atom?

The nucleus is tiny – only about one fifty-thousandth of the radius of the whole atom. If an atom could be blown up to the size of a football stadium, the nucleus would be the size of a can of baked beans in the middle. Even though it is so small, the nucleus makes up most of the atom's mass, or weight. The electrons surrounding the nucleus are very light in comparison, about one two-thousandth of the mass of a proton.

An atom with a nucleus the size of a baked bean would fill a stadium.

Atomic Theory

Who said "Atoms can neither be created nor destroyed"?

In 1807 the British chemist John Dalton produced a theory about atoms. He declared that everything is made of atoms, and that these cannot be created or destroyed. Scientists have since learned a lot more about the structure of atoms, but Dalton's ideas were the first steps toward modern atomic theory.

John Dalton

Who was Avogadro?

The Italian count Amedeo Avogadro (1776–1856) was a physicist and mathematician. He worked out that atoms formed substances by joining together to make molecules.

What are molecules?

A molecule is the smallest part of a substance that retains the nature of the substance. Take paper, for example. The thickness of each page of this book is roughly 100,000 paper molecules. If each paper molecule were broken up, it would no longer be paper, just a random group of atoms. Every molecule of a substance is made of the same number of atoms linked together in exactly the same pattern.

Who discovered the neutron?

The neutron (one of the elementary particles in the nucleus of an atom) was discovered in 1932 by the British physicist James Chadwick.

Water is made up of hydrogen and oxygen.

How many molecules are there in a teaspoonful of water?

The answer to this question gives some idea of how tiny molecules are. There are at least as many molecules in a teaspoon of water as there are teaspoonsful of water in the Atlantic Ocean.

Who first tried to weigh atoms?

The British chemist John Dalton (1766–1844) worked out that a molecule of water always contains the same proportions of oxygen and hydrogen. He thought oxygen atoms must be heavier than hydrogen atoms. In fact an atom of oxygen weighs 16 times more than an atom of hydrogen. He gave hydrogen the atomic weight of 1, because it was the lightest element.

What is the heaviest atom found in nature?

Uranium. Its atomic weight is 238, making uranium 238 times as heavy as hydrogen. Heavier atoms, such as plutonium (242) and lawrencium (257), can be made artificially, through nuclear reactions.

Who discovered electrons?

Electrons are grouped in "shells" around the nucleus of an atom. Electrons were discovered in 1897 by Sir Joseph John Thomson, working at Cambridge University in England. Thomson won the Nobel Prize for Physics in 1906 for his discovery.

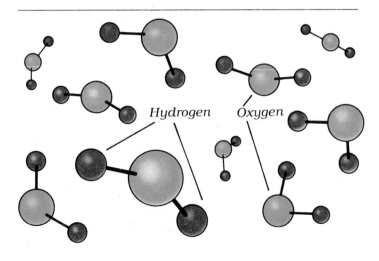

Hydrogen   *Oxygen*

Uranium

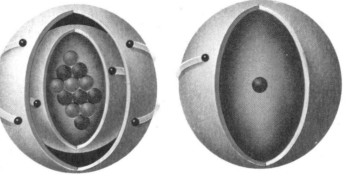

Carbon   *Hydrogen*

Electrons are arranged in 'shells' around the nucleus.

What are protons?

Protons are found in the nucleus of every atom. There are always the same number of protons in the nucleus as there are electrons orbiting around the nucleus. This number gives the *atomic number* of the element. Hydrogen, with one proton, has the atomic number 1. Carbon, with six protons, has the atomic number 6, and so on. Protons carry a positive electrical charge; electrons carry a negative charge.

Which is heavier, an electron or a proton?

A proton is much more massive than an electron – around 2,000 times heavier. Equally heavy is the neutron, the other main particle making up the nucleus. Neutrons carry no electrical charge.

Where are gluons thought to exist?

Gluons are thought to be tiny subatomic particles that hold quarks together. (Quarks are particles within the nucleus of the atom.) However, no one has yet proved that either quarks or gluons exist.

Who thought atoms were like plum puddings?

Until the early 1900s, nobody knew how the atom was arranged. Sir J. J. Thomson thought that the atom looked something like a plum pudding, with electrons scattered around like currants. Ernest Rutherford, in 1911, and Niels Bohr, in 1913, put forward different ideas.

Rutherford, a New Zealander, discovered the nucleus of the atom and proved that the electrons were very light. Bohr, a Danish physicist, devised the "sun and planets" model of particles orbiting the nucleus of the atom. This theory is accepted by most scientists today.

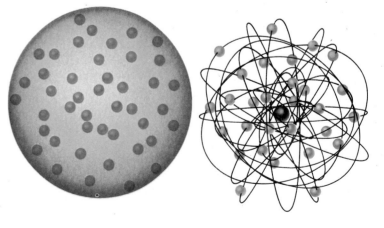

Thomson's model   *Rutherford's model*

Early theories of atom structure.

What is the quantum theory?

In 1900 the German physicist Max Planck showed that when a body gives off energy, this energy is radiated in "bundles," not as a steady stream. Planck called these bundles *quanta*.

Who applied quantum theory to atoms?

Niels Bohr reasoned that Planck's quantum theory could help to explain how atoms behave. He showed that electrons orbiting the nucleus of an atom give off energy only when moving from a larger orbit to a smaller one. The amount of energy given off is the quantum – the difference between the electron energies in the two orbits.

Which scientist formulated the famous equation E = mc²?

The formula was the work of the great scientist Albert Einstein. This is what it means.

When a neutron splits an atom, the mass of all the pieces is actually less than the mass of the original atom plus the neutron. How can this be? Because energy is released. Einstein's formula can be explained as follows: E = energy released; m = mass lost; c^2 = the speed of light squared. So the energy released in a nuclear reaction is equal to the mass lost multiplied by c^2. And c^2 is huge, for light travels at 186,000 miles a second! You can see, therefore, that even if the mass m is tiny, the energy E will be very great. The value of c^2 is 186,000 multiplied by 186,000! Try to work this out on your calculator.

Einstein's formula explains why such huge amounts of energy are released when the atom is split.

Niels Bohr

Energy

Electron

Nucleus

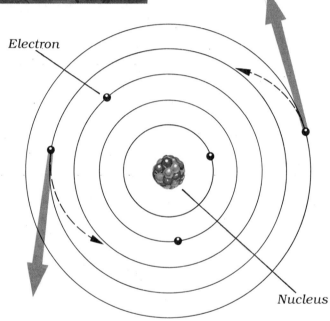

Electrons fall to lower orbits and give off energy.

Albert Einstein

Is there such a thing as antimatter?

No one has yet proved that antimatter exists anywhere in the Universe. But scientists think that logically it should exist. Just as matter is made up of particles (that form atoms), antimatter would be matter made up of antiparticles. An antiparticle would have the same mass as a known particle, but an opposite value. So the electron in an atom (which is negatively charged) would have as its antiparticle an equal but positively charged *positron*.

Atoms and Energy

Who first split the atom?

In 1919, a scientist did what the ancient Greeks thought impossible. He split the atom, and in so doing changed one substance into another. The man who did this was Ernest Rutherford, working at a British university. He bombarded atoms of nitrogen gas with alpha particles. This changed them into oxygen and hydrogen atoms.

Lord Rutherford

What is radioactivity?

A few of the heaviest atoms, being naturally unstable, can break down and change into other atoms. As this breakdown, or decay, takes place, radiation is given off. The French scientist Henri Becquerel discovered radioactivity in uranium in 1896. Radioactivity occurs in nature. It also happens when the atom is split by scientists. Radioactive rays are dangerous to health.

How is radioactivity measured?

The unit to measure the radioactivity of a substance is the becquerel (Bq), after the first scientist to discover radiation. Doses of radiation are measured in sieverts (Svs).

What are alpha and beta particles?

Anything that is radioactive gives off one or more kinds of rays, or particles; among the best known are alpha particles, beta particles, and gamma rays. Alpha particles are the nuclei of helium atoms. Beta particles are fast electrons. Gamma rays are a form of electromagnetic radiation.

How is radiation harmful?

Radiation is dangerous to health because it can affect the normal working of the cells in the body. This causes "radiation sickness" and can also lead to serious illnesses such as cancer and leukemia.

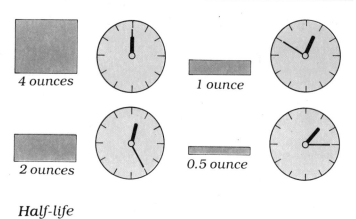

4 ounces

1 ounce

2 ounces

0.5 ounce

Half-life

What is meant by "half-life"?

Radioactivity occurs as the atoms in a substance break up, or decay. The half-life of a radioactive material is the time it takes for half of its radioactive atoms to decay. Different elements decay at different rates. Uranium 238 has a half-life of 4,510 million years – about the same as the age of the Earth. So about half of all the Earth's uranium has decayed into lead by natural radioactivity since the Earth was formed.

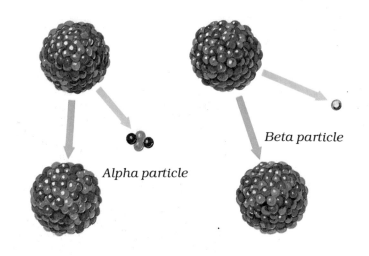

Beta particle

Alpha particle

Alpha and beta particles

Why is nuclear energy so named?

The word *nuclear* comes from *nucleus*, the core of the atom. When there is a change in the nucleus of an atom, energy is released. This is called nuclear energy. It is found naturally in the Sun and stars as well as on Earth. Scientists can also produce this energy in a nuclear power station or a nuclear weapon.

What is the difference between nuclear fission and nuclear fusion?

Both are kinds of nuclear reaction. In fission, a heavy nucleus (usually uranium) splits. In fusion, light nuclei fuse, or come together. Fusion produces a *thermonuclear* reaction and is the most powerful source of energy known. Nuclear fission is used in nuclear power stations and in atomic bombs. Fusion is used in hydrogen bombs and may one day be harnessed to provide unlimited power.

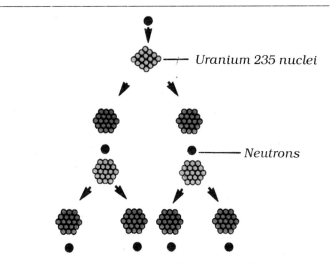

A nuclear chain reaction, the basis of the bomb.

What is a chain reaction?

When one event triggers another similar event, which in turn causes more of the same events, a chain reaction is taking place. When a neutron strikes a uranium atom, the atom splits. It also produces two or three "free" neutrons. These neutrons in turn strike other atoms and so on. This chain reaction, called fission, produces heat energy.

Who built the first nuclear reactor?

In 1942, Enrico Fermi was carrying out nuclear research at the University of Chicago in Illinois. In the university squash court he and Leo Szilard built the world's first atomic "pile," in which a chain reaction could be started and controlled. The pile was made of uranium blocks separated by graphite. Cadmium rods could be inserted into the pile to halt the reactor.

Why do scientists use uranium to produce nuclear energy?

Uranium is a fairly common metal and is naturally radioactive. One kind of uranium is the only element in which fission takes place easily, setting off a chain reaction. For this reason, it is the fuel used in nuclear power stations.

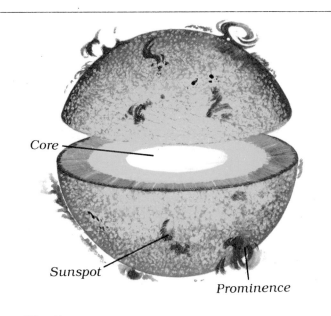

The Sun

What does the Sun have to do with nuclear energy?

Without the Sun's heat and light, there would be no life on Earth. The Sun's energy, like that of other stars, comes from nuclear reactions within its immensely hot interior. Hydrogen atoms combine to form helium in a fusion reaction which releases the Sun's life-giving energy.

Atoms at Work

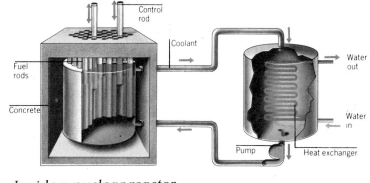

Inside a nuclear reactor

What happens inside a nuclear reactor?

Inside a reactor, uranium fuel is sealed inside rods. The rods are arranged in groups called fuel elements. A liquid (water or a molten metal) or a gas flows around the rods to cool them. Special control rods, made of a substance which absorbs neutrons, can be raised or lowered between the fuel elements. When lowered, these rods stop the chain reaction. As an extra precaution against neutrons escaping, the elements are surrounded by a "moderator" (again, water can be used). The moderator deflects neutrons back into the reaction. To contain the dangerous radioactivity produced by the chain reaction, the reactor assembly is shielded by thick walls of steel or concrete.

How does a reactor make electricity?

A nuclear power station works in the same way as an ordinary coal- or oil-burning power station, by heating water to make steam to drive turbines. The heat to make the steam comes from the enormous energy released by a chain reaction inside the station's reactor.

What is a breeder reactor?

Imagine a coal-burning power station that made more coal as it burned! In 1951 Walter Zinn designed a nuclear reactor that actually made its own fuel. Using uranium 235 as the fuel, the reactor produced heat for the generation of power. It also made as a by-product a new element called plutonium, which can be used for fuel in nuclear reactors.

How much power can a nuclear reactor generate?

A single nuclear reactor can produce as much heat as 40 million 100-watt lamps.

The radiation from the Chernobyl explosion spread over much of Europe.

What happened at Chernobyl?

In April 1986 there was an accident at the Chernobyl nuclear power station in the USSR. A reactor exploded and radioactive gases spilled out into the air. Large areas of countryside were contaminated by the radioactivity, which affected plants and animals. People living around the damaged power station were moved to new homes. The reactor itself was too dangerous to repair and it was sealed in concrete. It will remain sealed for many years – possibly forever.

When were atomic bombs first dropped on cities?

The first atomic bombs were dropped during the Second World War (1939–45). Allied scientists had discovered how to start a chain reaction and create an explosion many times more powerful than any previous explosive. The first atomic bombs were dropped on the Japanese cities of Hiroshima and Nagasaki in 1945. Each bomb had a destructive power equal to 22,000 tons of high-explosive TNT. Both cities were destroyed and more than 200,000 people were killed. Many more people died later from the effects of the deadly radiation. Dropping the A-bombs made Japan surrender and so brought the war to its end.

What is the difference between an atomic bomb and a hydrogen bomb?

An atomic bomb gets its energy from nuclear *fission*. The hydrogen bomb gets its energy from nuclear *fusion* and is known as a *thermonuclear* weapon. An ordinary A-bomb must be exploded first to generate the enormous heat needed to set off an H-bomb.

What is the most powerful nuclear weapon?

An A-bomb's explosive power is measured in kilotons. One kiloton equals 1,000 tons of TNT. Much more powerful is the H-bomb. Its explosive power is measured in megatons. One megaton equals one million tons of TNT. The most powerful H-bomb known to have been tested was a Soviet weapon of 60 megatons exploded in 1961.

An underground nuclear test

Why is nuclear waste dangerous?

Nuclear power stations produce waste, some of which is contaminated by radiation. When an old nuclear power station is shut down, all the parts affected by radiation can be dangerous. So too is the waste left over after used fuel elements have been "reprocessed" to make new ones.

How can we get rid of nuclear waste?

Getting rid of nuclear waste is difficult, particularly because the effects of radiation take many years to disappear. One way is to bury waste underground. Another is to dump it at sea. The waste must first be sealed in containers, so that no radioactive material can leak out to contaminate the environment. The most dangerous waste is sealed in glass and left to cool down. Cooling will take at least 50 years. One safe way might be to get rid of it in outer space.

A barrel containing highly dangerous nuclear waste.

Will there one day be nuclear-powered spacecraft?

There are already satellites orbiting the Earth which use nuclear power to provide the electricity for their instruments. Today's spacecraft use chemical fuel rockets. For future voyages to the planets and beyond, nuclear engines capable of working for years without refueling may be needed.

What is an isotope?

Nearly all elements have atoms of two or more different weights. Atoms that belong to the same element, yet have different weights, are called isotopes. For example, hydrogen has three isotopes, called protium, deuterium, and tritium.

What are isotopes used for?

Some radioactive isotopes are useful in industry and medicine. For instance, the radiation from the isotope cobalt 60 is used instead of X-rays to take photographs through metals and so detect cracks and other faults. Radioactive isotope scanning is used by doctors to study the workings of people's internal organs.

Who might wear a nuclear pacemaker?

A person whose heart is not working properly can be helped by nuclear energy. A device called a pacemaker is fitted to the patient's body. It sends out electrical impulses which keep the heart beating regularly. The power for the pacemaker can be supplied by a tiny nuclear power unit.

What is a Geiger counter?

This device detects and measures radiation, such as alpha particles and gamma rays. It can be used by geologists to find uranium-bearing rocks. The Geiger counter was invented by Hans Geiger in 1908.

What does a particle accelerator do?

Scientists use particle accelerators (called cyclotrons and synchrotrons) to study charged particles. The accelerator is like a giant racetrack in which the particles are accelerated to very high speeds by a magnetic field. Then they are shot out to hit a nucleus. The first cyclotron was made by the American physicist E. O. Lawrence in 1931.

Why can nuclear submarines stay at sea for such a long time?

A nuclear submarine is driven by turbine engines which use steam heated by a nuclear reactor. The submarine seldom has to return to port to refuel. The world's first nuclear-powered submarine was the US Navy's *Nautilus* (1955). A lump of uranium fuel the size of an electric light bulb provided enough energy to drive the submarine 62,137 miles. In 1960 the US nuclear submarine *Triton* sailed around the world under water – a distance of 41,632 miles – in three months, without needing to refuel.

A nuclear submarine

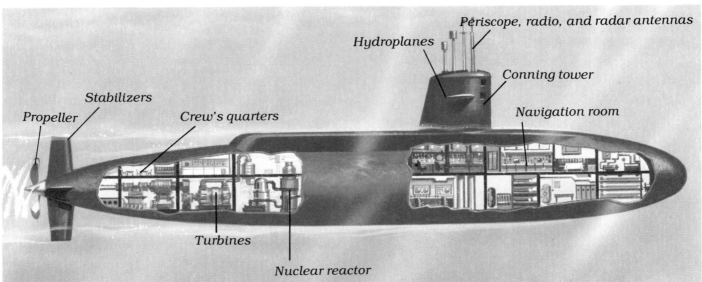

Periscope, radio, and radar antennas

Hydroplanes

Conning tower

Navigation room

Stabilizers

Propeller

Crew's quarters

Turbines

Nuclear reactor

THE ELEMENTS

What is an element?

An element is a substance made up of only one kind of atom. All the atoms in an element have the same atomic number, and it is impossible to break up an element into parts that have different chemical properties.

How many elements are there?

There are 92 elements found in nature. Others can be made only in the laboratory during atomic reactions. In all, 109 elements have been isolated.

Which are the most common elements on Earth?

The most common element in the Earth's crust is oxygen (about 50% by weight). Next comes silicon (about 28% by weight).

Oxygen is the most abundant element on Earth; much of it is in the oceans.

Which is the rarest element?

The rarest element in nature is astatine. It is produced when radioactive uranium decays. Astatine can be made artificially, but it is very unstable.

What is a mineral?

Most chemical elements react with other elements so readily that they are not found singly, or uncombined, on Earth. Instead, they combine (join) with one another as minerals. Some 3,000 minerals are known.

What was the "universal element"?

The Greek philosopher Thales, who lived around 600 B.C., thought all matter was made of water, the universal element. Heraclitus, about 500 B.C., thought the universal element was fire. Other thinkers believed it was air. It was Aristotle (384 to 322 B.C.) who argued that there were four elements: fire, air, earth, and water.

What did medieval alchemists mean by the term *element*?

In the Middle Ages, alchemists believed that all matter was made up of three so-called prime movers, or elements. These were salt, sulfur and mercury. They thought gold was made of "pure" mercury and "clean" sulfur. Less precious "base" metals were believed to contain "unclean" sulfur.

Alchemists in the Middle Ages dreamed of turning base metals into gold.

What was the philosopher's stone?

The alchemists dreamed of finding a way to change base metals, such as lead, into pure gold. For this, they believed it was necessary to use a magical third substance, the "philosopher's stone." Their search was fruitless, for no such magic stone exists.

When were most elements discovered?

Some elements, such as copper, gold, and iron, have been known since prehistoric times. But most were not isolated (discovered in their pure form) until the last 200 years. By 1830 about 50 elements were known. Elements 93 to 109 were not discovered until after 1940.

Tutankhamun's gold mask made in 1352BC.

What is the periodic table of elements?

In the 1860s scientists realized that there were "family likenesses" between certain groups of elements which behaved in similar ways. They arranged these groups into a table, known as the periodic table. The Russian chemist Dmitri Mendeleyev set out the table in 1870. There were gaps, but he was sure that unknown elements must exist to fill these gaps, and so it has proved. The periodic table has 18 vertical columns, or groups. These similarities are repeated periodically in the horizontal rows, making seven "periods."

Mendeleyev, Cavendish and Davy

Do any elements not fit the periodic table?

Two series of elements are shown at the foot of the periodic table, and behave a little differently. Elements 57 to 71 are known as the rare earth or lanthanide elements. Elements 89 to 103 are known as the actinide series.

Who was Henry Cavendish?

In 1766 Henry Cavendish (1731–1810), an English nobleman with a passion for science, discovered hydrogen. This new gas was so light that it afterward gave rise to the first aviation experiments with balloons. Cavendish also discovered that water was composed of hydrogen and oxygen.

How many elements did Humphry Davy discover?

The English chemist Sir Humphry Davy (1778–1829) discovered these six elements: boron, sodium, magnesium, potassium, calcium, and barium. He is probably best known for inventing the miner's safety lamp which is named after him.

Which is the most recently discovered element?

Element number 108, named unniloctium, was discovered in 1984. Its name means "108," and it was actually identified after element 109, named unnilennium.

How are elements named?

Some elements are named in honor of their discoverer. For example, polonium was named after Poland, in honor of the Polish-born scientist Marie Curie, who discovered the element. Others have Greek or Latin names, or are named after the place where they were first found.

Why are elements given symbols?

Scientists use a form of shorthand to save time and space when writing the names of elements. Each element has a symbol. There is never more than one capital letter in the symbol, and this makes it easier when writing out long chemical formulas. Examples are oxygen (symbol O), helium (symbol He), and silver (symbol Ag, from the Latin word *argentum*, meaning "silver"). Why could silver not be simply S or Si? Because S is the symbol for sulfur and Si stands for silicon.

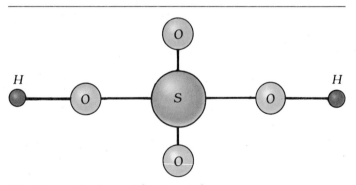

The formula for sulfuric acid.

How are chemical formulas written?

A chemical formula is a code to show the composition of a substance. For example, the formula for sulfuric acid is H_2SO_4. This shows that each molecule of sulfuric acid contains two hydrogen atoms, one sulfur, and four oxygen atoms.

States of Matter

What are the three states of matter?

The three states in which matter exists are solid, liquid, and gas. Solids have both shape and volume; their molecules are held together tightly. Liquids have volume too, but no shape; their molecules are held together less tightly, so that a liquid will flow into a container. Gases have neither volume nor shape; their molecules are free to move about, and a gas will fill any container which encloses it.

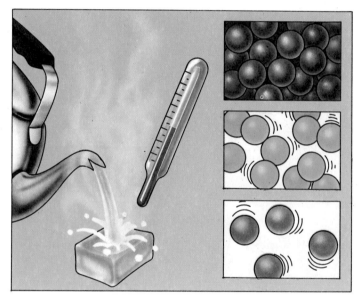

Water can exist as solid (ice), liquid (water), or gas (water vapor). Molecules act differently in each state as shown here.

Can matter change its state?

Many substances change state quite easily when heated or cooled. Water is a liquid at normal temperature but changes to a gas (water vapor) when heated. When water is cooled, it becomes a solid (ice).

Are all minerals solids?

Of the 3,000 known minerals, all but two are solids. The two exceptions are mercury and water, which are liquids.

Can you see a gas?

Most gases are invisible, because their molecules are spread so thinly. A gas can be changed into a liquid by being cooled, when it becomes visible.

How do liquids behave in space?

Astronauts in space must take care not to spill their drinking water. The liquid forms spheres, because the water molecules attract each other equally and pull the liquid into a perfectly symmetrical shape, but there is no gravity to make them fall. Tiny globules of water float freely like bubbles inside the spacecraft and can be very hard to clean up!

Why are raindrops pear-shaped?

On Earth water droplets are not spherical because gravity pulls the liquid spheres out of shape. Watch a dripping faucet and you will see that the drops are pear-shaped. Raindrops are the same, pulled out of shape as they fall toward the ground.

Weightless, in space, an astronaut's orange juice would float out of the cup.

What is weightlessness?

The body becomes weightless when in "free fall" in space. An astronaut in an orbiting spacecraft can float in a weightless state; so (for a short time) can people inside an aircraft flying a special *parabolic* flight path.

What is evaporation?

When a liquid is heated, it will change to a vapor. The steam coming from a boiling kettle is water vapor; a gas. The same thing happens when hot sun shines on a wet road: water vapor can be seen rising. This is evaporation. Evaporation can be used to extract salt from salty water. Boiling causes the water to evaporate as vapor, and solid salt crystals are left behind.

Glass blowing

Is glass a solid?

Glass is best described as a congealed (hardened by cooling) liquid. A true solid has a definite melting point, when it becomes a liquid. But when glass is heated, it just gets softer and softer without having a definite melting point.

Boyle's Law: if the temperature remains constant and the volume halves, the pressure of a gas always doubles.

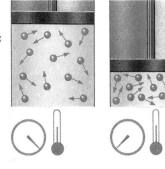

What is Boyle's law?

In 1662 Robert Boyle discovered an important fact about the way certain gases behave. It is this: If the temperature remains constant (the same), the gas inside a container will halve in volume when the pressure on it is doubled. If the pressure is halved, the volume of the gas doubles.

Why does a balloon burst when you squeeze it?

If you blow up a balloon and then squeeze it, the volume of air inside is reduced, and its pressure increases. Eventually the pressure of air inside becomes so great that the balloon bursts. This is a practical demonstration of Boyle's law.

Why does a half-filled balloon fill when placed in hot sunlight?

The more a gas is heated, the greater its volume becomes. Test this yourself on a summer's day. Blow into a balloon until it is half full, tie the neck, and put the balloon in the Sun. As the Sun's heat warms the air inside the balloon, it expands and the balloon will begin to fill. This is a demonstration of another "gas law," discovered about 1787 by the French scientist Jacques Charles. Charles's law states that, provided the pressure remains constant, the volume of a gas will double if the temperature is also doubled.

How are crystals formed?

Crystals are solids found in nature in an almost endless variety of sizes and shapes. Most solid matter, including nearly all minerals and metals, are crystalline. You can watch crystals form in a sugar solution. If you add sugar to water, the sugar dissolves to make a sugar and water solution. If you heat the solution to boiling point, the water will begin to evaporate. The remaining solution will contain more and more sugar. Eventually, the water that is left will be "saturated" with sugar and the sugar will begin to form crystals.

Calcium sulfate crystals which form the fur in a kettle.

How many sides does a snowflake have?

Our word *crystal* comes from the Greek *krystallos*. The Greeks examined frost and snow and saw patterns in them. A snowflake is a crystal of frozen water. Seen through a microscope, snowflakes reveal many beautiful forms. But each flake has the same number of sides, or branches: six. Snowflakes are *hexagonal* (six-sided) crystals. Scientists group all crystals into six families, according to their symmetrical shapes.

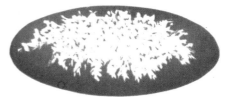

Dissolve some sugar in water: as it evaporates sugar crystals will form.

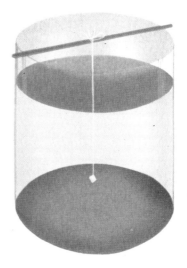

Make a strong salt solution and attach a thread as shown. A salt crystal will form on the thread.

Why are all solids elastic?

After a solid is struck, it will slowly regain its former shape. This is known as elasticity. The most common elastic objects are rubber bands (which stretch) and balls (which bounce). But in fact every solid is elastic to some degree. Otherwise, the world would be very curious, for every object would slowly alter in shape as it was touched or struck by other objects.

Chemical Reactions

What is a chemical reaction?

When two or more substances are put together, they may mix, as when you mix sand and water in a bucket, but remain separate substances. However, if a chemical reaction takes place, they may undergo a chemical change and become a different kind of substance. For example, when zinc is added to sulfuric acid, a reaction occurs. The products are hydrogen gas and zinc sulfate.

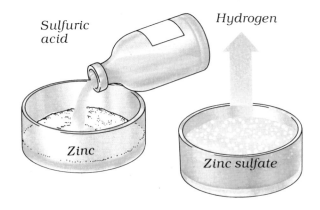

Sulfuric acid

Hydrogen

Zinc

Zinc sulfate

A simple chemical reaction

What is a compound?

A compound is a substance made up of two or more elements which cannot be separated by physical means. For example, water is a compound of hydrogen and oxygen. Each water molecule is made up of two hydrogen atoms joined to one oxygen atom by invisible forces called bonds.

How does a compound differ from a mixture?

Salt water is a mixture of two compounds, salt and water. It is easy to separate the two by boiling the water, which evaporates, leaving salt crystals behind. It is much more difficult to split water or salt into their elements; it can be done only by forcing an electric current through them. A mixture can easily be separated; a compound cannot.

Can all elements form compounds?

All but six elements combine with other elements to form compounds. The six "outsiders" are gases: helium, neon, argon, krypton, xenon, and radon. They are in one group of the periodic table and are known as the inert or noble gases because they do not combine with other elements to form compounds as the other gases do.

What is meant by chemical change?

A substance can be changed chemically by heating. When heated, chalk changes to lime and carbon dioxide gas. A substance can also be changed by combination with another substance. For example, the elements copper and sulfur will combine to form a compound, copper sulfide, when heated together.

What is a catalyst?

A catalyst is a substance which speeds up a chemical reaction without itself being changed. For example, nickel can be used to aid the reaction of hydrogen with carbon monoxide to make methane and carbon dioxide.

What is combustion?

Combustion is a chemical reaction between a gas and another substance. When iron combines with oxygen in the air it rusts; this is slow *oxidation*. Burning is another more violent form of oxidation, producing both light and heat. Combustion cannot take place when no air is present.

Why does a flame need two gases to keep burning?

When a gas burns, it produces a flame. But to keep burning a flame needs another gas to support the combustion. In a lighted candle, the paraffin wax changes to a vapor (gas) which needs oxygen from the air to keep burning. Cover the candle with a glass jar and the flame will go out because it has used up all the oxygen from the air inside.

Why does iron get rusty?

This is an example of a chemical combination between the iron present in a car's body and frame and the oxygen in the air. The product of this reaction is iron oxide, or rust.

Rust is red iron oxide.

Why is some water hard and other water soft?

The "hardness" of water is caused by the presence of calcium and magnesium salts. Hard water does not lather easily when you wash in it with soap. Soft water is free of the salts, and soap easily forms a lather. One way to soften hard water is to add sodium carbonate.

What was soap made from in early times?

Soap made from animal fat and wood ash was used thousands of years ago. Wood ash was a source of alkali. Soap making depends on a chemical reaction between fat and the alkali. The ingredients were heated in a vat to make a putty-like mass. Soap making was a messy business and people often complained about the smell.

How do detergents clean clothes?

Detergents do not contain soap. They are made from petrochemicals which come from coal and oil. They work because they have molecules with "water-attracting" heads and "water-repelling" tails. The tails pull away from water, sticking to the clothes and the dirt on them. The heads pull away from the material into the water, taking the dirt with them.

Medieval soap making

What did Lavoisier discover?

Antoine Lavoisier, who lived from 1743 to 1794, was a French scientist and one of the founders of modern chemistry. His most important discovery was that matter cannot be destroyed during a chemical reaction, even though it may change its appearance. This is one of the basic laws of science: the law of conservation of mass. It means that the amount of matter produced by a chemical reaction must always be the same as the amount that took part in the reaction. Lavoisier was executed by the guillotine during the French Revolution.

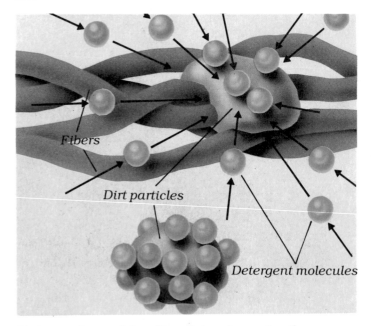

Detergents work by dissolving in water then attracting the oil-soluble dirt particles.

Carbon Chemistry

What is organic chemistry?

Organic chemistry has to do with the compounds containing the element carbon. About 95 percent of all known compounds contain carbon. Inorganic chemistry is concerned with the compounds of other elements.

Why are there so many carbon compounds?

Carbon is the only element with atoms which are able to join together to form chains, rings, and other more complicated bonds. This means that there is a huge number of organic (carbon) compounds; nearly four million are known.

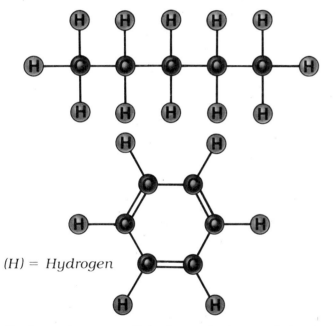

(H) = Hydrogen

Carbon atoms can form long chains and rings.

Where is carbon found?

Carbon is found in the rocks of the Earth, in substances such as coal, petroleum, and limestone. As a gas (carbon dioxide) it is found in the atmosphere, and it is also found dissolved in water. Carbon exists on the Sun and also in the atmosphere of other planets in the solar system.

What are diamonds made of?

Diamond is a form of carbon. It is the hardest substance known. Natural, uncut diamonds look dull and have little luster. The brilliant gems that are so valuable are made by careful cutting and polishing.

A diamond, made from carbon is the hardest known substance.

What is the lead in a pencil made of?

The so-called lead in a pencil is not lead at all but graphite, another form of carbon. Graphite is so soft that it marks anything it touches.

How much carbon dioxide is there in the air?

There is very little, about three parts in ten thousand. Yet this small amount is vital, as plants need it to live. Carbon dioxide is found dissolved in water and can be extracted from rocks such as limestone.

What compound is a shellfish's shell made of?

The shells of sea creatures such as cockles and whelks are made from carbon compounds called carbonates. Carbonates are compounds of carbon, oxygen, and a metal. Some limestone deposits are made up almost entirely of the shells of long-dead shellfish.

Sea shells are made of calcium.

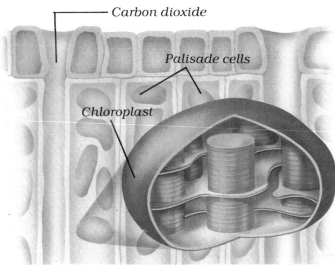

Carbon dioxide

Palisade cells

Chloroplast

Site of photosynthesis

Plants use the process of photosynthesis to produce food. Photosynthesis takes place in the leaf which is shown above in cross section.

Which chemical process is essential to all plant and animal life?

A process called photosynthesis enables green plants to grow. The plant uses energy from sunlight and a chemical agent called chlorophyll to turn carbon dioxide and water (from the air and soil) into sugars and oxygen. The plant feeds on the sugars and releases the oxygen into the atmosphere. No animal life could exist on Earth without this process taking place constantly.

What are carbohydrates?

Carbohydrates are compounds made up of carbon, hydrogen, and oxygen. They are made in plants during the process of photosynthesis (see previous question). The three main types of carbohydrate are sugars, starch found in foods such as cereals and potatoes, and cellulose.

What is the carbon cycle?

All plants and animals use carbon compounds. Animals breathe in oxygen and breathe out carbon dioxide. Plants use carbon dioxide in photosynthesis, and in turn release oxygen. More carbon dioxide is given off by decaying matter and burning.

Acids, Bases, and Salts

What is an acid?

An acid is a chemical compound containing hydrogen and at least one other element. For example, sulfuric acid (formula H_2SO_4) is made up of hydrogen (H), sulfur (S), and oxygen (O). Acids are normally found as liquids.

Which acids can we eat?

Certain acids, known as organic acids, are found in food plants. For instance, citric acids are found in lemons and oranges, and malic acid is found in apples, plums, and rhubarb.

Vinegar and citrus fruit contain acids.

Why are some acids dangerous?

Some acids are so strong that they burn skin and even dissolve metals. In concentrated form, such acids must be handled with great care. When diluted with water, they are less harmful. Some acids can even eat through glass, and so must be kept in special containers.

Strong acid will burn skin and dissolve metal.

Which is the most widely used acid?

The acid most useful in industry is sulfuric acid. It can be made cheaply in many different ways. One of its uses is in the manufacture of fertilizers. Another name for sulfuric acid is oil of vitriol. It was known to Arab scientists as long ago as the eighth century; they wrote of it as a powerful "dissolving spirit."

How can acid remove the "fur" inside a tea kettle?

The inside of a tea kettle or water tank may become "furred" by chalky deposits of calcium carbonate. Most acids will dissolve carbonates, so the solutions sold to clean the insides of kettles contain a weak acid. This dissolves the chalk, and carbon dioxide gas bubbles are given off.

How can you test for acid?

A simple test for an acid is to dip into the liquid a piece of blue litmus paper—paper stained with a blue dye that responds to the presence of acid. If acid is present, the litmus paper will turn red.

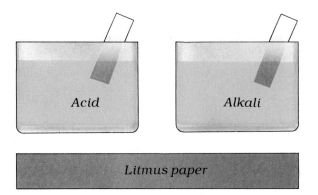

Litmus paper turns red in acid and stays blue in alkali.

Which acid helps digestion?

Hydrochloric acid (HCl) is a very powerful acid, which in concentrated form is used to clean metal. A small amount of weak hydrochloric acid is present in the body's gastric juices. These juices help to digest food in the stomach.

What is aqua regia?

Aqua regia is a mixture of concentrated hydrochloric acid and nitric acid. It is so powerful that it will dissolve any metal, except silver. Because it could attack gold and platinum (thought of as the purest of metals) it was given its name, meaning "royal water."

Which acid is found in peach stones?

Very small amounts of prussic acid are found in the stones of peaches and also in almonds. This acid contains cyanide, which is one of the most deadly poisons known. It smells like bitter almonds (though not every person can detect the smell).

What is a base?

A base is a substance which reacts with an acid to form a salt-plus-water. Most bases are the oxides or hydroxides of metals; in other words they are the products of reactions with oxygen or hydrogen. One of the most easily remembered chemical rules concerns acids and bases. It is this:

Acid + Base = Salt + Water

When this happens, the acid and base are said to *neutralize* each other.

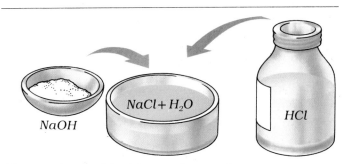

How sodium chloride can be made.

How can common salt be made?

When hydrochloric acid (HCl) combines with sodium hydroxide (NaOH) (a base), what happens? Acid and base neutralize each other to form common salt (sodium chloride) and water. This is the chemical formula for the reaction:

Acid   Base   Salt   Water

$$HCl + NaOH = NaCl + H_2O$$

Metals

What is a metal?

Elements can be divided into two basic groups: metals and nonmetals. Metals can be made to shine or have a luster, they conduct heat and electricity easily, and they are "malleable" – they can be beaten into shape or pulled out into wire. More than 70 of the known elements are metals.

What is an alloy?

An alloy is a mixture of metals or of metals and another substance. Copper, for example, is a pure metal and an element. When copper and tin (also a pure metal) are mixed together by heating them until they melt, they make an alloy called bronze.

Bronze was one of the first alloys discovered. These bronze spears are nearly 2000 years old.

Which two metals make brass?

Brass is an alloy of copper and zinc. It has been used since early times, and brass musical instruments are mentioned in the Bible.

Where are metals found?

Metals are found in the earth, though seldom in their pure form. Gold, platinum, and some copper and silver are found in their pure state, but all other metals occur as ores.

What is an ore?

An ore is a substance containing not only metal but also other materials such as oxygen, sulfur, and carbon. These other substances must be removed, by heating or by *electrolysis*, to obtain the pure metal.

What is meant by the relative density of a metal?

The term *relative density* is a convenient way to describe the heaviness of metals. Iron has a relative density of 7.8. This means that it is 7.8 times as heavy as water.

Archimedes' famous experiment proved that the King's crown was not pure gold.

Which metal is named after the Devil?

Nickel, an easily shaped and polished metal, derives its name from Old Nick, an old term for the Devil. Copper miners in Germany found ores that they could not reduce to workable copper and they called these copper-like ores *Kupfernickel*, meaning "devil's copper." The unknown substance causing the trouble was actually another element, now known simply as nickel.

Why is sodium hard to handle?

Sodium is one of the so-called alkali metals. It reacts violently with water, forming a substance called a hydroxide and giving off hydrogen gas. Sodium reacts with almost all compounds, including oxygen, and so has to be stored away from the air, often under kerosene.

Panning for gold

Which are the heaviest and lightest metals?

The heaviest metal is osmium, with a relative density of 22.5. The lightest metal is lithium, which has a relative density of 0.5.

Where was the world's largest gold nugget found?

Gold is found in the earth in all sizes, from tiny grains to large nuggets. The largest lump of gold ever found was the Welcome nugget, found in the Ballarat goldfield in Australia in 1858. It weighed 182 pounds.

Which metal most easily conducts heat and electricity?

Silver has the highest conductivity of all known metals. It is also valued for its beautiful appearance. Because it is easily worked and has a bright, light-reflecting finish, it has been used since ancient times for making coins and ornaments.

Which is the most abundant metal on Earth?

The metal found most plentifully in the Earth's crust is aluminum, which makes up about 8 percent of the crust. It is found not as a pure metal but as an ore called bauxite.

Silver conducts electricity better than any other metal.

Which island gave its name to a metal?

Copper, a metal known since prehistoric times, takes its name from the island of Cyprus in the Mediterranean. The Romans called the metal *aes Cyprium,* meaning "bronze of Cyprus," because they obtained most of their copper from the island.

Cyprus gave its name to copper.

Which metals give color to fireworks?

People who make fireworks know that certain metals will give off different colors when the fireworks are burned. Strontium gives red, sodium yellow, barium green. Magnesium gives fireworks their brilliant white light.

Which metal is found in chalk?

Calcium, a soft, white metal, is rarely found in its pure state. It occurs as calcium carbonate in chalk, limestone, and seashells, and as calcium sulfate in gypsum and alabaster.

What is potash?

This is another name for potassium carbonate, which was first made by dissolving wood ash in water and boiling away the liquid in a pot. This process gave it the name potash, which is used as a fertilizer.

Why is the metal potassium no good for making cooking pots?

Potassium combines easily with many substances and so hardly ever occurs naturally in its pure state. It is very soft and will float on water. If potassium is dropped into water, it releases the hydrogen in the water, which burns with a red-blue flame. Potassium has to be kept covered with oil to keep it from reacting with the air.

A spectacular fireworks display

Potassium explodes in water.

What is galvanizing?

Galvanizing is a means of preventing iron and steel from corroding by coating them with zinc. Zinc will not corrode, or rust. Bridges such as the Golden Gate in San Francisco are made from galvanized steel.

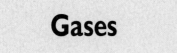

Gases

What is the air around us mostly made of?

About 78 percent (by volume) of the air is nitrogen. About 21 percent is oxygen. Carbon dioxide, water vapor, helium, and other gases make up the rest.

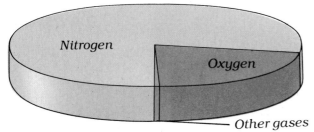

The composition of the atmosphere

Why is oxygen important?

Oxygen makes up about one fifth of the Earth's atmosphere. It is a colorless, odorless gas. Plants produce oxygen by photosynthesis. Animals need oxygen to keep them alive. They take in oxygen by breathing and use it to break down their food to produce energy.

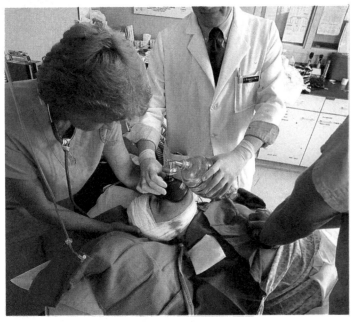

A patient receives vital oxygen after an accident.

What is liquid air?

If air is cooled under pressure to around minus 328 degrees Farenheit, it becomes a colorless liquid. As the liquid warms, each gas present boils at a different temperature and can be extracted in its pure state.

What is ozone?

Ozone is what is termed an *allotrope* of oxygen. It is made up of oxygen atoms combined in threes, so its chemical formula is O_3. It behaves differently from oxygen, but gives the same products in chemical reactions. When ozone is heated, it quickly turns into oxygen. It dissolves in water much more readily than oxygen does.

Gay-Lussac in a balloon over Paris

Who went up in a balloon to study the air?

The French chemist Joseph Louis Gay-Lussac (1778–1850) discovered that the air is the same mixture at different heights, although its pressure, temperature, and moistness decrease the higher you go. He carried out his experiments in balloons flying over Paris.

What is methane?

Methane gas is a compound of carbon and hydrogen. It is chemically the same as the natural gas piped into homes for heating and cooking. Another name for methane is marsh gas.

Why is carbon monoxide harmful?

Carbon monoxide is a very poisonous gas which has no color or smell. It is found in coal gas and in the exhaust fumes of car engines.

Why will carbon dioxide put out fires?

Carbon dioxide gas will not support combustion. If sprayed on a fire from a fire extinguisher it forms a blanket, cutting off the oxygen which would otherwise feed the flames.

Carbon dioxide foam is used to smother flames.

What is dry ice?

Dry ice is the name given to solid carbon dioxide. Normally, this is an invisible gas found in the air. Under pressure, the gas turns into a liquid and then when the pressure is reduced, a snowlike solid appears. This is called dry ice. It is useful for keeping things cold, particularly because as it warms up it sublimes, or turns to vapor, without first melting and leaving puddles.

Modern airships are filled with helium, which is not as light as hydrogen but cannot catch fire.

Which gas is most suited for use in balloons and airships?

Hydrogen is the lightest gas and was used in early balloons and airships. But it has the great disadvantage of being highly inflammable and several large airships have exploded with great loss of life. Helium is second to hydrogen in lightness. Because helium does not catch fire, it is much safer and is used in modern lighter-than-air craft.

What are the inert gases?

Helium and five other gases (neon, argon, krypton, xenon, and radon) are found naturally only in very small quantities. They are "inert"; that is, they do not easily react with other substances to make compounds. They occupy about one percent by volume of the air, and are called the "noble" gases.

Which gas is used to purify swimming pools?

Chlorine kills disease-carrying bacteria and so is added to the water in swimming pools. Chlorine has a strong smell and is greenish-yellow in color. Its name comes from *chloros*, the Greek word for green.

Which gas makes drinks fizzy?

The bubbles in fizzy drinks are carbon dioxide gas.

Dissolved carbon dioxide makes drinks fizzy.

Which gas smells of rotten eggs?

One of the most horrible-smelling gases is hydrogen sulfide. It produces the "stinkbomb" smell.

Which gas is called "laughing gas"?

A gas once used by doctors and dentists as an anesthetic had the unusual side-effect of making patients laugh. It was nitrous oxide (also known as dinitrogen oxide, N_2O). The chemist Humphry Davy tested the gas on himself to find its effects.

Which gas was detected in the Sun before it was found on Earth?

Helium was detected in 1868 by a scientist studying the light from the Sun. The gas's name comes from the Greek word for the Sun, *helios*. It was not found on the Earth until 1895!

There is more hydrogen than any other element in the whole Universe.

Which is the most abundant element in the Universe?

There is no rival to hydrogen, which is found in large amounts in the Sun and is also present in the stars and the nebulae, or gas clouds, between the stars. Yet very little pure or "free" hydrogen occurs on Earth; there is less than one part per million in the atmosphere. Hydrogen exists all around us, however, combined with oxygen, carbon, and other elements in water. Without it, there would be no life as we know it on Earth.

ELECTRICITY

When did the electrical revolution begin?

Human life changed dramatically when scientists discovered how to harness the mighty power of electricity. Without this revolution, which began in the late 1700s and gathered speed during the 1800s, our lives would be very different. We would have no radios or televisions, no telephones, no computers. Our streets and homes would still be lit by gas lamps and we would have none of the gadgets that we take for granted today.

What is electricity?

Electricity is a form of energy. It is produced when electrons—tiny atomic particles—move from one atom to another. Although scientists had known that this mysterious energy existed, its workings were not understood until the secrets of the atom began to be revealed about a century ago.

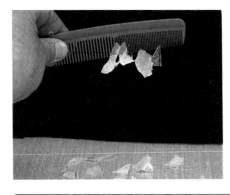

You can pick up bits of paper after combing your hair because of the static electricity on the comb.

How did electricity get its name?

Around 600 B.C. the Greek thinker Thales of Miletus found that rubbing a piece of amber caused it to attract pieces of cork or feather. Our word *electricity* comes from the Greek word *elektron*, meaning "amber."

Benjamin Franklin flew a kite in a thunderstorm to demonstrate the electricity in lightning.

Where is electricity found in nature?

Electricity is everywhere, but it is seen most dramatically in a lightning flash, which is a huge electric spark in the atmosphere.

Who proved that lightning was electric?

In 1752, the statesman and scientist Benjamin Franklin determined to find out if electricity and lightning were connected. He carried out a very dangerous experiment. He took a kite and attached to it a metal rod. Then he tied the end of the kite string to a door key and went out into a thunderstorm. When he flew the kite into a thundercloud, he saw sparks flash and felt a shock as electricity from the cloud passed from the kite down the string to the key.

How do lightning rods protect tall buildings?

Lightning may strike tall buildings as well as trees during a storm. To prevent damage to the building the electricity must be led away to the ground. From a metal rod on top of the building, a wire leads the electricity down to earth. Benjamin Franklin tested the first lightning rod shortly after his famous kite-flying experiment in 1752. Today all tall buildings are fitted with lightning rods.

How can objects be electrically charged?

All matter is made up of atoms. Normally, each atom has the same number of electrons and protons (*see page 5*). The *positive* charge of the protons and the *negative* charge of the electrons cancel each other out. But if this balance is upset, the object becomes electrically charged. For example, if a balloon is rubbed with a cloth, electrons pass from the cloth to the balloon. The balloon becomes negatively charged, and the cloth, having lost electrons, becomes positively charged. Unlike charges always attract each other, so the cloth clings to the balloon.

Rubbing a balloon with a cloth produces static electricity.

What is an electric field?

Any object which is electrically charged has around it an area called an electric field. Inside this field the electrical charge can be detected.

What was a friction machine?

In the 1600s, scientists found that they could produce an electric charge with a machine. By turning its handle, they could spin a large ball of sulfur. If a person put his hand on the ball as it turned, this produced friction which charged the ball with electricity. Eventually the ball would contain enough charge to give an unsuspecting person a shock.

What is a conductor?

A conductor is a material through which electricity can pass. Electricity travels more easily through some materials than others. Metals are good conductors of electricity. Lightning rods are made of copper, an excellent conductor.

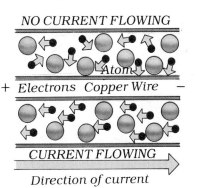

NO CURRENT FLOWING

Atom

+ Electrons Copper Wire −

CURRENT FLOWING

Direction of current

Electrons pass from one atom to the next to conduct electricity.

Why are metals such good conductors of electricity?

Most metals contain many free electrons, able to move from atom to atom. This makes them good conductors of electricity (and also heat). Substances such as plastic, glass, and rubber have few free electrons and so are poor conductors.

Are metals the only conductors of electricity?

Silicon and graphite (which are nonmetallic substances) are also conductors. So is water, especially if salt or acid are added. Animal and plant tissues conduct electricity because they have a high water content.

What are superconductors?

When made very cold, certain substances have almost no resistance to electricity; they become superconductors. This was first observed in 1911 using mercury. More than 25 other metals, including copper and various alloys, behave in the same way. Superconducting coils that allow current to flow practically nonstop are used in "particle accelerators." New materials that may superconduct at room temperature are being developed.

Part of a superconducting coil

What is an insulator?

An insulator is a material that will not conduct electricity. Good insulators are diamond, glass, paper, plastic, rubber, and many gases. That is why the wires inside an electrical cable are enclosed in a rubber or plastic sheath. The plug on the end of the wire is also made of rubber or plastic. The insulating material protects us from getting a shock when we touch the cable or the plug.

How does electricity travel?

If you put six dominoes in a line, flat and end to end, you can do an experiment to see how electricity moves along a wire. Each domino must touch the next one. Draw back the lead domino and tap it sharply against the next in line. Watch what happens. Each domino moves just a little, except for the end one, which shoots away. The electrons in a wire move in the same way. When one end is "pushed" by an electrical force, each electron in the wire moves just a little, but together they send a fast and powerful signal along the wire.

What is an electrical circuit?

In order to flow, a current must be able to find its way around a circuit. For example, if you connect a wire from one terminal of a bell to a battery, you must also connect another wire from the second terminal back to the battery. The circuit is now complete and the bell will work.

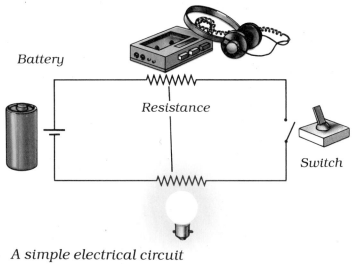

Battery

Resistance

Switch

A simple electrical circuit

What is meant by electrical resistance?

An electric current is pushed along a wire by the force of the power source (such as a battery). But it is also held back by *resistance* in the circuit to the free flow of electrons. Poor conductors of electricity offer a high resistance to the flow of current. Resistance is measured in units called *ohms*.

Why are there at least two wires inside an electric cable?

Electricity needs two wires to make a circuit. One wire carries the current from the plug to the appliance; the other wire takes the current back to the plug, and finally back to the power station.

How fast does electricity travel?

When you switch on an electric light, the bulb glows almost at once. The electric signal travels from the switch through the wire to the light almost as fast as light itself. That is a speed of 186,000 miles a second.

What pushes an electric current along?

Electricity was once thought to be an invisible fluid. This is why we use the word *current* to describe its movement. The force within an electrical source (such as a battery) that moves the current along is called the *electromotive force*, or EMF for short. This force is measured in *volts*. The strength of the current itself is measured in *amperes*, or *amps*.

What causes electricity to move?

Imagine two connected water tanks, placed level side by side. No water will flow between them, because the pressure is the same. If one tank is raised, the pressure balance alters and a current of water will flow from the higher to the lower. A similar difference in "pressure" or EMF makes an electric current flow. The difference is known as the *potential*.

James Watt is remembered by the unit used to rate light bulbs—the watt.

What does James Watt, of steam engine fame, have to do with electricity?

The power of electricity is measured in *watts*. This unit was named after the Scottish engineer James Watt (1736–1819), pioneer of the steam engine. The watt is a unit of work rate. Most electrical goods are marked with a power rating in watts. A light bulb, for example, may be 60 or 100 watts; an electric heater may be two kilowatts (2,000 watts).

What is meant by AC and DC?

When electricity flows continuously in the same direction, it is known as *direct current* or DC. The electricity in a flashlight flows in a direct current. *Alternating current*, or AC, changes direction all the time. It builds up to maximum strength in one direction, decreases to nothing, and then builds up to maximum strength again, but in the reverse direction. Then again it decreases to nothing. This action is called a cycle of flow. The number of cycles in one second is called the *frequency* of the current.

Pylons carry electricity around the country.

Which is most useful, AC or DC current?

A current that constantly changes its direction of flow does not sound easy to use, but in fact AC current is. It is easy to change, or transform, the voltage of AC current to make it larger or smaller. DC voltage is more difficult to transform. AC current can be easily converted to DC. It is less simple to change DC to AC.

What kind of current runs into our homes?

The wires in our homes carry alternating current. AC current can be sent long distances through cables at very high voltages with little power loss. The voltage must be reduced before we can use it. In America domestic electricity is supplied at between 120 and 220 volts. The AC current repeats its cycle 60 times every second.

Storing and Making Electricity

What was a Leyden jar?

The Leyden jar was an early device for storing electricity. Scientists found that they could store electricity from a friction machine (*see page 31*) by leading it down a wire into a bottle of water. When they held the bottle and touched the wire, they received a shock stronger than the shock they felt from the machine itself. This proved that electricity was being stored in the bottle. Putting tin foil inside and outside the bottle improved its storage qualities. This discovery was made in the Dutch city of Leyden in the mid 1700s. Modern devices for storing electricity are called condensers.

Galvani

Who thought that frogs could make electricity?

In 1786 an Italian scientist named Luigi Galvani found that dead frogs twitched when connected to an electrical friction machine. When frogs' legs were hung from a metal railing, they also twitched. Galvani thought that the nerves and muscles of the frog must contain an electrical power that caused the dead limbs to move.

Galvani was wrong. He had used brass hooks to hang the frogs' legs from the iron railings. The two metals, not the frogs, were reacting chemically and producing electricity, and the legs (being moist) were acting as conductors. Unknowingly, Galvani had discovered the principle of the electric cell.

Who made the first battery?

Alessandro Volta (1745–1827) realized why Galvani's frog experiment worked. Using zinc and copper disks separated by damp paper he made, in 1799, a "cell" that produced an electrical current. By standing several cells in a pile, he discovered that he could produce a stronger current. Volta improved his "voltaic pile" by using an acid or salt solution instead of water to moisten the paper. He had made the first battery.

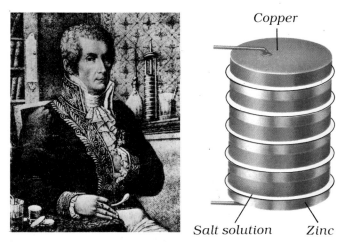

Copper

Salt solution   *Zinc*

Volta discovered the first way to store electricity.

Why was Volta's invention so important?

Volta demonstrated his battery to Napoleon in 1801 and was made a count by the delighted French emperor. Volta's reward was deserved. He had found a way of producing a steady supply of electricity. Friction machines gave people shocks and produced exciting displays of sparks, but they were of little help to the serious study of electricity. Using Volta's battery, scientists were able to discover much more about electricity and electromagnetism.

What is a simple electric cell?

A simple electric cell can be made by placing a copper rod and a zinc rod into a solution of sulfuric acid. The rods are the cell's *electrodes*. The acid is the *electrolyte*. When a wire is connected between the electrodes, an electrical current flows between them. Put several cells together and you have made a battery.

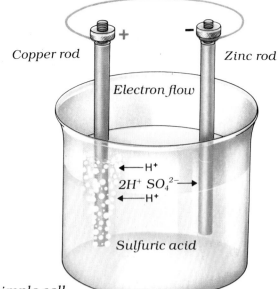

A simple cell

What chemistry goes on inside the simple cell?

The molecules of sulfuric acid solution split into positively charged (+) hydrogen ions and negatively charged (−) sulfate ions. The zinc electrode gives off zinc ions, leaving it with more electrons than protons. The extra electrons flow through the wire to the copper electrode. This gives the copper rod a negative charge. Unlike charges attract each other, so the negative copper rod attracts hydrogen ions from the acid. Bubbles of hydrogen gas collect on the copper rod.

What are ions?

An ion is an atom, or group of atoms, carrying an electrical charge. Ions carry the electric current between the electrodes of a cell. A positive (+) ion is formed when an atom loses one or more electrons. A negative (−) ion is formed when an atom gains one or more electrons.

What is electrolysis?

Electrolysis takes place when an electric current passes through a liquid. For example, if a current passes through water, hydrogen and oxygen can be separated. The positive electrode is called the *anode* and collects negatively charged oxygen. The negative electrode is called the *cathode* and collects positively charged hydrogen.

How is electrolysis used?

Electrolysis can extract pure metals from their molten (liquid) ores. It is used to produce aluminum from bauxite ores, and also to extract magnesium from the magnesium chloride salt in seawater.

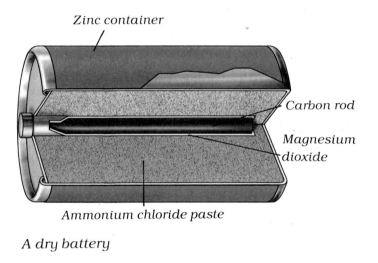

A dry battery

What is a dry battery?

A dry battery is the kind you use in a flashlight. It has a zinc case (negative), and inside is a chemical paste surrounding a carbon rod (positive). So it is not really dry at all; the paste has enough moisture to allow the cell to work.

How does a car battery work?

The car battery is an example of a secondary cell, or accumulator. It can be recharged when it begins to run down by connecting it to an electrical supply. When recharged, the battery's chemistry works just as when it was new. Most car batteries have lead-acid cells.

Why are nickel-cadmium batteries useful?

The nickel-cadmium battery can be recharged like an accumulator, but is much smaller and can be used in an electric razor, for example. The battery contains an electrolyte of potassium hydroxide, a positive electrode of nickel hydroxide and nickel oxide, and a negative electrode of cadmium.

Magnetism

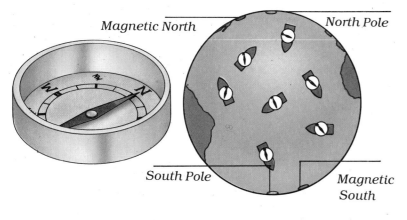

A compass will always point toward the magnetic North Pole.

What is a magnet?

A magnet is a piece of metal with the power to attract other substances. Iron and steel make good magnets. A magnet has two *poles*, north and south, near to its ends. Unlike poles (north and south) attract each other, just as opposite (+) and (−) electrodes do. Like poles (north and north, south and south) repel each other. Try putting two bar magnets together and watch what happens. Can you tell which are the magnets' like poles?

What gave magnetism its name?

The power of lodestone was thought to be magical. Its attraction was named magnetism by the Greeks, after a district in Macedonia called Magnesia, where lodestone was common.

When was the compass first used in history?

Knowledge of the magnetic compass traveled slowly from China to Arabia, and from the Arabs it passed to Europe. European sailors were using simple compasses in the 1100s. They placed a magnetized iron needle on a pivot and watched to see in which direction it swung.

Which is the world's biggest magnet?

The Earth itself acts as an enormous magnet. It has north and south magnetic poles (which are not the same as the geographic poles). The first person to suggest that the Earth is magnetic was William Gilbert, court physician to Queen Elizabeth I, in 1600. We now know that every large spinning body, such as a planet, has a magnetic field.

Which is more powerful, a bar magnet or a horseshoe magnet?

A horseshoe magnet will lift about three times as much weight as a bar magnet of the same size. This is because the attractive power of its two poles is combined by their being close together.

Why do magnets have keepers?

A magnet tends to lose its magnetism gradually, unless a keeper is used. The keeper is a piece of soft iron put across the poles of a horseshoe magnet or connecting the north pole of one bar magnet with the south pole of another magnet.

How did the Chinese use the lodestone to help them find their way?

In ancient times people discovered that the lodestone (an ore now known as magnetite) could attract small pieces of iron. If a bar made from lodestone was spun, it always swung to face north. This strange behavior made the lodestone valuable as a direction finder—the first magnetic compass. The Chinese are said to have used lodestone compasses as early as 2000 B.C.

An early European compass invented 3,000 years after the Chinese discovered lodestone.

Who discovered electromagnetism?

In 1820 a Dane, Hans Christian Oersted, discovered the *magnetic effect*. He was working with a battery and an electrical circuit, when he noticed that every time he brought a wire through which current was flowing near a magnetic compass, the compass needle jumped. When he disconnected the wire from the battery, the compass needle returned to normal. Oersted's discovery that magnetism and electricity were closely connected, and that one could produce the other, was of immense importance.

How do magnetism and electricity differ?

Magnetism and electricity are alike in many ways, something realized by early scientists. One important difference is that the force between two magnetic objects is not affected by the material that separates them. The force between two electrically charged objects is affected by whether the separating material is a good or poor conductor.

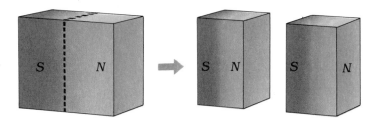

Magnetic poles stay the same even if the magnet is broken.

What happens if you cut a magnet in half?

If you cut a bar magnet in two, each half becomes a new magnet, with its own north and south poles.

What is magnetic induction?

If you hang a steel pin from a magnet you will find you are able to make a chain of pins. Each pin is magnetically attracted to the one above. Remove the first pin from the magnet and the invisible link is broken. The pins were held together by magnetic induction.

How can you make a magnet?

A magnet is made up of many molecular magnets called dipoles. Before a piece of iron is magnetized, all the tiny magnets inside are jumbled up. Their magnetic forces cancel one another out. To magnetize a piece of iron, you must rub it gently (in one direction only) with a magnet. This lines up all the tiny magnets in the iron, so that all the north poles point one way and all the south poles the other way. Steel is better than iron, because it retains its magnetism longer.

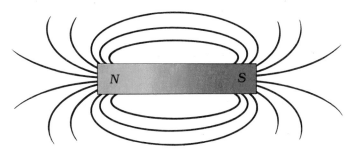

Magnetic fields

What does a magnetic field look like?

Around every magnetic object are invisible lines of force streaming out in all directions. This "magnetic field" can be seen by doing a simple experiment with some iron filings, a piece of thin cardboard, and a magnet. Sprinkle the filings onto the cardboard, and place the magnet underneath. Tap the cardboard gently and you will see the filings arrange themselves in a pattern. Look closely at the way the lines form around the poles of the magnets, where the field is strongest.

Using Electricity and Magnetism

When were electromagnets first made?

In the early 1800s the French scientist André Ampère tried passing an electric current through a large coil of wire. He found that the coil then behaved like a magnet, with north and south poles. In 1825 an Englishman named William Sturgeon tried placing an iron rod inside a coil and discovered that this greatly increased the power of the magnet. As early as 1830 electromagnets able to lift weights of more than 2,000 pounds were in use.

Powerful electromagnet

Which former errand boy became a great British scientist?

Michael Faraday was born in 1791. He was a blacksmith's son and had little schooling. At ten years old he was working as an errand boy for a bookseller. Reading the books gave him his first taste for science and he went to hear a lecture by the famous chemist Sir Humphry Davy. Faraday wrote to Davy and eventually went to work for him as his assistant. This set Faraday on the path to his own brilliant scientific career.

Michael Faraday

How did Faraday invent the dynamo?

In 1831 Michael Faraday turned Oersted's discovery of the magnetic effect ten years earlier to a use. He reasoned that if electric current could produce magnetism, then magnetism ought to produce electricity. He found that if a magnet was brought toward or away from a coil, or if the coil was moved to and from the magnet, an electric current was produced. As the magnet's force field was cut by the wire, a current was *induced* in the wire. This is the basic principle of both the dynamo and the electric motor.

How does an electric motor work?

An electric motor works in the opposite way to a dynamo. It turns electrical energy into mechanical energy. An armature is a coil fixed on an axle between the poles of a magnet. When the current is passed through the coil, the armature will rotate and keep moving for as long as the current continues to flow.

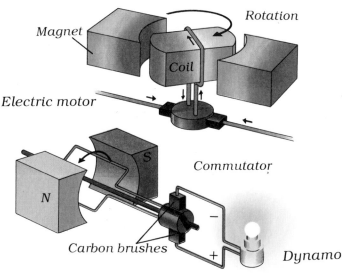

Magnet   *Rotation*

Coil

Electric motor

Commutator

N   *S*

Carbon brushes

Dynamo

How does a simple dynamo work?

A dynamo is a generator that turns mechanical energy into electrical energy. It has an armature (a coil able to spin on its axis) positioned between the poles of a magnet. When the armature turns, a current flows in the coil each time it crosses the force field of the magnet.

Where does our electricity come from?

The electricity that we use at home, at school, and at work is made by giant generators, or dynamos, in power stations. These stations are of two main kinds. The first kind, called a thermal power station, converts heat into electricity. It works by burning fuel to boil water to produce steam. The steam drives turbine generators. The fuel may be oil, coal, or nuclear fuel (uranium). The second kind of power station uses the energy of moving water to drive the generators and is called a hydro-electric power station.

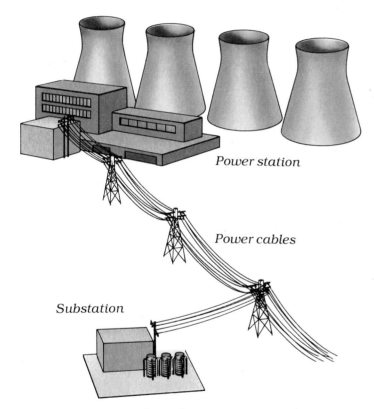

Power station

Power cables

Substation

The major parts of an electric power system

How is electricity carried across country?

At a power station, the electricity produced is boosted to a high voltage, or pressure (for example, 400,000 volts) by transformers. Having such high voltages allows relatively thin cables to carry a lot of current over long distances. The transmission lines are either buried underground or hung from tall towers called pylons. The network of supply lines forms an electricity grid across the land.

How does electric current get to our homes?

It is not safe to allow a 400,000-volt current leaving a power station to enter our homes. So the power is greatly reduced at substations for transmission through cables beneath city streets, and finally to 120 or 220 volts (in the US) for use in the home. Inside each building is a main switch which controls the flow of current, and a meter to measure the amount of electricity used by each customer.

How can a high voltage be changed to a smaller one?

Voltages can be made smaller or larger by passing current through a transformer. A transformer is made by winding two coils of wire around an iron core. One coil, the primary coil, is made of thick wire but has a few windings only. The other, the secondary coil, has many windings of much thinner wire. A voltage passed through the primary coil is changed, or transformed, when it passes through the secondary coil. The voltage may be increased (stepped up) or decreased (stepped down), depending on the number of winds on each coil.

How does a switch work?

A switch is used to open or close an electrical circuit. When the switch is on, it connects the circuit so that current flows. When the switch is off, the circuit is broken and no current can flow.

Why does an electrical wire grow hot?

The heat is caused by electrons bumping into the atoms of the metal conductor in the wire. All conductors resist the flow of electricity to some extent. The best conductors offer least resistance. Copper is the metal most commonly used in electrical wiring. It is cheaper than silver, although not quite such a good conductor. Even copper wire will become warm if a current is passed along it for a long time.

How does a fuse act as a safety device?

A fuse cuts off the electricity supply in a circuit when something goes wrong. Inside the fuse is a thin wire, able to carry a safe amount of current but no more. If an electrical appliance, such as a hair dryer, overheats it will start to use more electricity. When this happens, the thin wire in the fuse (usually in the plug) heats up too and, being thin, the wire melts. This breaks the circuit and so cuts off the electricity supply.

When were electric lights first used?

Electric light replaced gaslight from the 1880s. Joseph Swan of Britain (1878) and Thomas Alva Edison of the United States (1879) each invented an electric lamp.

What makes a light bulb glow?

The thin wire, or filament, inside a light bulb is a resistance to the flow of current through it. When electricity is passed through the bulb, the filament becomes hot and glows brightly. To keep the filament from burning away completely, the glass bulb is filled with a mixture of inert gases (usually argon and nitrogen). The filament in most modern light bulbs is made of tungsten.

What is photoelectricity?

When light strikes certain substances, an electrical effect is produced. The energy of the light rays separates electrons from the atoms of the substance. This electricity is called photoelectricity.

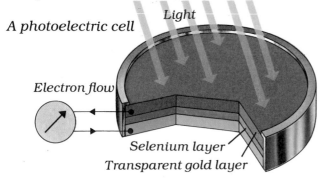

A photoelectric cell

Light

Electron flow

Selenium layer

Transparent gold layer

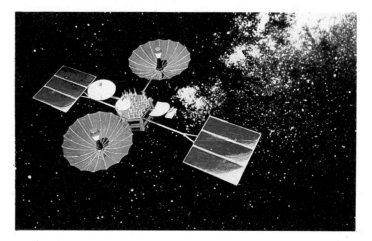

Satellites use solar wings to generate electricity.

How do spacecraft make electricity from sunlight?

Spacecraft have batteries of cells, called photovoltaic cells, which convert the Sun's energy into electricity. Each "solar cell" produces only a tiny amount of electricity, so large numbers are required for each spacecraft. The cells are usually arranged as panels on extending wings. Solar panels can also be used on Earth to heat houses and swimming pools.

How do "electronic eyes" work?

The "magic eye" that automatically opens a door as you approach, or operates a burglar alarm, is worked by photoelectricity. A beam of light shines on a photoelectric cell. When the beam is interrupted (by someone walking through it) the cell activates an electrical circuit. The circuit may start a motor to open a door or (in a burglar alarm) set off a bell.

Why should you never touch anything electrical when you are wet?

Never touch anything electrical, such as a light switch, if your hands and feet are wet. Water conducts electricity and allows electric current to flow into your body more easily. The electricity in your house can give a shock powerful enough to cause serious injury or death. So anyone handling electrical wiring or appliances should always take care and follow sensible safety rules.

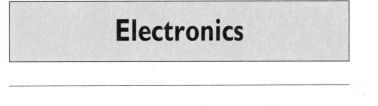

Electronics

What are electromagnetic waves?

The energy given off by the acceleration of an electric charge travels in the form of waves. The waves produced by electric and magnetic fields travel at right angles to each other and to the direction in which the waves travel. In a vacuum, the *electromagnetic waves* travel at the speed of light. How a changing magnetic field could cause a changing electrical field was set out in precise mathematical terms by the scientist James Clerk Maxwell (1831–1879).

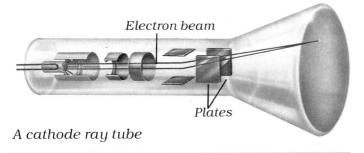

A cathode ray tube

When were cathode rays first studied?

In the 1800s scientists became interested in the behavior of electricity in air at low pressure. They experimented with glass tubes from which most of the air had been pumped out. When a strong electric current was passed through the tube between two metal electrodes, a bright glow was produced. At very low pressure the glass tube itself gave off a greenish light. This was because rays were being given off from the cathode (the negative electrode). The glass tubes were called cathode ray tubes.

How can current flow through a gas?

Electrons can be made to flow through gases, liquids, or even a vacuum. This fact made possible the electronic revolution. To make a current flow outside a conductor (such as a wire), the electrons must be forced away from their atoms. This can be done in three ways: by heat, by light, or by hitting the atoms with other electron "bullets."

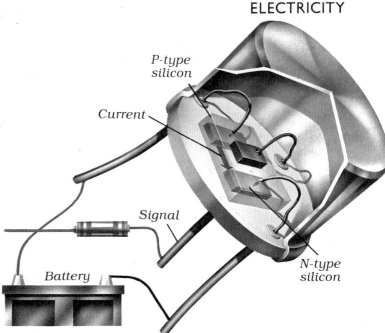

Transistor, made from semiconducting silicon

Who invented the first vacuum tube?

An electron or vacuum tube is made of glass. Inside a simple vacuum tube are two electrodes—a cathode that gives off electrons and an anode that attracts electrons. The electrodes are connected to a plate wired to the base of the tube. The simplest form of vacuum tube is the diode, invented by Ambrose Fleming in 1904. It passes current one way only and can be used to detect radio signals.

What is a triode vacuum tube?

The triode vacuum tube was invented by Lee De Forest in 1906. It was an improvement on the diode because it could also amplify, or strengthen, signals. The triode made possible the development of high-quality radio receivers, television, radio telescopes, and radar.

Why was the transistor so much better than the electron tube?

The transistor was an important advance on the vacuum tube. It was invented by three Americans (named William Shockley, John Bardeen, and Walter H. Brattain) in 1948. The new device was much smaller than a tube, more difficult to damage, and it used less power because it had no glowing filament. A small current in one part of the transistor can control a larger current in another part.

What are transistors made of?

Transistors are made of materials called *semiconductors*. These materials will conduct electricity, though not as well as metals. They fall halfway between conductors and insulators. A common semiconductor material is silicon.

What is an integrated circuit?

An integrated circuit is a complicated arrangement of transistors and other components on a single piece, or chip, of semiconductor material. The first one was made in 1958. Making circuits smaller and smaller allows an incredible amount of electronic power to be contained in a tiny space. Hundreds of electronic components can be fitted into an integrated circuit the size of a letter in this sentence.

How are microchips made?

First, a pattern of the components is drawn onto a large sheet. Then it is transferred, reduced many times in size, onto a thin disk of silicon. The silicon is baked in a furnace with other materials which are absorbed into its surface to form the pattern of components. Further layers are then added to complete the "sandwich" which makes up the finished microchip.

Why do microchips work so quickly?

Inside a microchip, the components are crammed together into a very tiny space. Electrical charges can move between them in almost no time at all, so the chip does its work at amazing speed.

Microchip

Computers

Who designed the first computer?

The English mathematician Charles Babbage (1792–1871) was the pioneer of the computer. He designed a huge calculating machine, called the Analytical Engine, which in theory could be programmed to carry out various mathematical operations. It was so far ahead of its time that it could not be built. There was no way of providing enough power to the Analytical Engine's thousands of cogwheels and other moving parts.

ENIAC—the first modern computer

What was the first real electronic computer?

ENIAC, completed in 1946 at the University of Pennsylvania, was the world's first computer which could do many mathematical tasks. ENIAC is short for Electronic Numerical Integrator and Calculator.

When did the computer age begin?

The computer age really began during World War II (1939–45). British scientists built a machine called Colossus to crack German secret codes. Colossus was a *dedicated* computer: breaking codes was the only job it could do.

How many generations of computers have there been?

The first-generation computers contained vacuum tubes, like an old-fashioned radio. The second generation, in the late 1950s, contained transistors. In the 1960s came the third generation, with integrated circuits. In the 1970s appeared the fourth generation, with LSI or Large Scale Integration (microchips holding lots of tiny transistors). Each generation has been smaller but more powerful than the one before. Soon we shall see the fifth generation of computers, which will be able to "think" for themselves.

Cray 2—a supercomputer

What is a mainframe computer?

A mainframe computer is the kind used by big businesses and government departments. The only type that is larger is called a supercomputer.

What is a microcomputer?

Microcomputers are the kind we use at home and in school. They are no bigger than a television set and they are useful for teaching, for small businesses, and for playing computer games.

How does a computer use its memory?

A computer has four main parts. It has a central processing unit or "brain." It has an input unit that feeds in data (usually linked to a keyboard), and an output unit that produces finished work (for example, as a printout on paper). The fourth and vital part is the memory unit, where the computer stores the information it needs to carry out its work. The computer stores this data on magnetic disks.

Can you bend a floppy disk?

The information needed to run a microcomputer is stored on small magnetic disks (or less often nowadays on cassette tape). The disks are called floppy disks. They are made of plastic, coated with a magnetic material, and they are encased in plastic for protection—so you can't bend them. Much more data can be stored on "hard" disks, and these are used in larger computers.

What is a computer program?

All computers need sets of instructions to tell them how to carry out their work. This information comes in the form of a program, which must be entered into the computer before it will work.

The components of a modern microcomputer

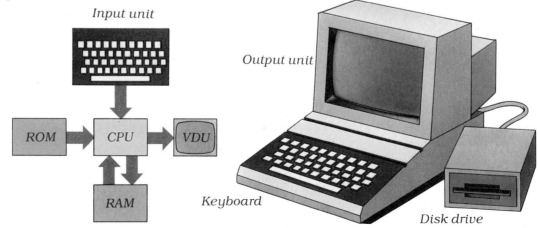

Input unit

Output unit

Keyboard

Disk drive

ROM — CPU — VDU
RAM

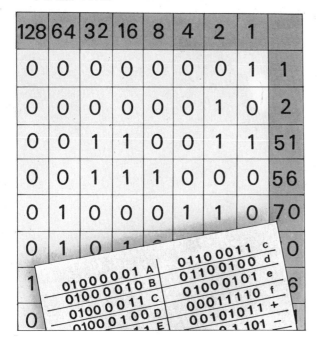

128	64	32	16	8	4	2	1	
0	0	0	0	0	0	0	1	1
0	0	0	0	0	0	1	0	2
0	0	1	1	0	0	1	1	51
0	0	1	1	1	0	0	0	56
0	1	0	0	0	1	1	0	70

Binary code

Why do computers have their own languages?

The data a computer needs is given to it in the form of a program written in a special language. A simple computing language used in home computers is BASIC (short for Beginners All-purpose Symbolic Instruction Code). There are many others.

What are software and hardware?

Software is another name for computer programs— either the ones you buy (such as games) or the ones put into the computer by the manufacturer. Hardware is the computer "machinery" itself, including the keyboard, screen, and printer.

Can you eat ROM and RAM chips?

In a computer's memory, data is stored in "binary" code on microchips. There are two kinds of memory chip. ROM (standing for Read-Only Memory) chips hold permanent programs that the computer needs to work and which cannot be changed. RAM (short for Random-Access Memory) chips hold just the program and data which are needed to do one particular job.

Where would you find bits and bytes?

All computers use binary code, a way of counting using only two values: 1 (on) and 0 (off). These represent the ons and offs of electrical voltages. The space needed for a binary 0 or 1 is known as a binary digit, or bit. A byte is a group of eight bits (usually enough space for a number or letter).

How is a computer's memory measured?

The capacity of a computer's memory, or the size of a computer program, are measured in K. K stands for kilobyte, and one K is equal to 1,024 bytes.

What will the "superchip" be made of?

The world's most powerful supercomputer, the American Cray 3, will have semiconductor chips made of a material called gallium arsenide which will conduct electrons up to ten times faster than silicon. It will work perhaps twelve times as fast as the most powerful supercomputers now in use, and should be able to perform 16 "gigaflops" (that is 16 billion operations) a second!

How do bar codes work?

In a supermarket, the checkout clerk "reads" each item in your cart electronically by scanning the pattern of black and white stripes marked on the package. This pattern is the bar code, containing information which is passed automatically to the store's main computer. In this way, each sale can be individually recorded as a sale at the checkout and the store knows how many of each item has been sold.

Where would you find an LCD?

LCD stands for liquid crystal display, and you would find one on a calculator or a digital watch.

Robots

How do robot factory workers learn their jobs?

Robots can do some jobs better than people can. They will go on repeating tasks, without ever becoming tired or bored. To learn a new task, the robot's brain must be shown how the job is done. A human moves the robot's "arms" and "hands" through each stage (of a car assembly, for example). The robot memorizes each step and, when it has been shown them all, it will work on its own. Before it can be given a new job, the robot's memory must be wiped clean.

How do aircraft rely on electronics?

Modern high-speed aircraft are packed with electronics. Electronic aids look after navigation, watch the engines' fuel consumption, and carry out safety checks on the plane's systems. An autopilot can take over from the human pilot, keeping the aircraft flying on course and at the correct height and speed. Some advanced warplanes depend on electronics just to stay in the air. Onboard computers make constant adjustments so that the plane can fly aerobatic maneuvers at very fast speeds.

The complex instrument panel on board the space shuttle

The robots R2-D2 and C-3PO from Star Wars

Will there ever be bionic people?

In science fiction stories, a bionic person is someone with superhuman strength and brainpower "added on" by electronic surgery. Fiction is already becoming fact, as doctors learn how to replace human organs with electronic spare parts. People suffering from heart disease can be helped by electronic pacemakers and even artificial hearts.

What is an android?

An *android* is a human-like robot. Androids may be built one day to do work too dangerous for humans. But there is really no advantage in making a robot look like a human.

What will the electronic homes of the 21st century be like?

In the next century homes could be very different from ours today. A central computer could run all the home's systems, such as heating, lighting, air conditioning, water supply, door locks, and so on. The computer will control all the domestic gadgets and communication systems, such as television, radio, and telephone. It will order goods to be delivered from local stores and check the family car. People will be able to work from home, using computer links to exchange information with friends on the far side of the world.

LIGHT AND SOUND

What is light?

No one really knows what light is made of. In the 1600s Isaac Newton thought light was made up of bullet-like particles he called *corpuscles*. The Dutch scientist Christiaan Huygens thought light was made up of pulses, or waves, traveling through space. Modern science has found some truth in both theories. Light certainly does travel in waves, but it also behaves as if it were made of particles. Scientists now call these light particles *photons*.

Is light energy?

Light is a form of energy and is similar to heat. It is the only type of energy that we can see directly. A blazing fire radiates heat and light. We can only feel the heat, but we can see the light.

Where does light come from?

Light comes from stars, such as our Sun. Stars shine as a result of their immense nuclear energy. Because the Sun gives off light, it is said to be *luminous*. Very few things are luminous, but among them are some animals such as fireflies and deep-sea fish which have light-producing organs.

How fast does light travel?

Light travels at enormous speed, at roughly 186,000 miles a second (300,000 kilometers a second). At this speed, the light from the Sun still takes more than eight minutes to reach the Earth.

Who first measured the speed of light?

The Italian scientist Galileo attempted to measure the speed of light in the early 1600s. He stood two men with flashing lamps on distant hilltops and tried to measure the time it took the light to travel between them. But light could not be measured like this: it travels much too fast. In 1676 Ole Roemer of Denmark measured how long it took light from the planet Jupiter to reach the Earth and came up with a figure for the speed of light that is almost the same as that calculated by modern scientists.

A firefly can produce its own light.

Does the Moon make its own light?

The Moon has no light of its own. What we see as moonlight is simply the reflection of the Sun's light from the Moon's surface. Without the Sun, we could not see the Moon at all.

What are light waves?

If you throw a pebble into a pool, it sends out ripples of waves. Light also travels in waves. In 1873 the scientist James Clerk Maxwell discovered the wave structure of light after 20 years' research. He showed that light is made up of vibrating waves of electrical and magnetic fields. The vibrations take place at right angles to the direction of the wave's motion and to each other. Maxwell was the first to suggest that light was a form of *electromagnetic radiation*. He went on to state that other kinds of rays must also exist, invisible to the eye.

Why is it dangerous to look at the Sun?

The Sun is an immensely powerful source of light. Our eyes are very delicate and easily damaged. You should never look directly at the Sun, not even through smoked glass or sunglasses. The Sun's rays are powerful enough to damage the retinas of your eyes and blind you.

What makes us cast a shadow?

Light travels in straight lines. If an opaque substance, such as a human body, is in the way, the rays are blocked. If you put your hand in front of a flashlight, a shadow will form on the wall. Watch what happens when you move the flashlight slightly to the side. On a sunny day see where your shadow is around noon and mark the outline with a piece of chalk. Try the same experiment in the late afternoon, when the Sun is lower in the sky. What has happened to your shadow?

What is an eclipse?

An eclipse happens when one heavenly body prevents the Sun's light from reaching another body. When the Earth moves between the Sun and the Moon, it casts a shadow and darkens the Moon. This is a lunar eclipse. Sometimes, the Moon passes between the Earth and the Sun, and for a short time day becomes night. This is a solar eclipse.

Plants do not develop if left in the dark.

Why is light so vital to life on Earth?

All life depends on sunlight. Plants could not grow without it, and without plants animals could not exist. The sense human beings rely on most is eyesight. Our eyes give us more than 80 percent of the information that our brains receive.

Why can we see through glass?

A sheet of clear glass is *transparent*; it allows light rays to pass through, so our eyes can see through it. A substance that blocks light, such as wood or metal, is said to be *opaque*. Waxed paper allows some light to pass through, but you cannot see shapes clearly. The paper is *translucent*.

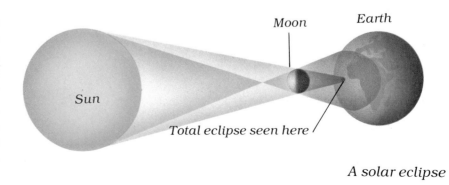

A solar eclipse

What makes light bend?

Light is bent when it is reflected, or bounced back, from a surface, such as a mirror. This bending is called *reflection*. Light is also bent when it travels from one transparent surface to another. This bending is called *refraction*.

Why does a stick standing in a pond look bent?

If you poke a stick into a pond, the stick will appear to bend at the point where it enters the water. This bending is caused by refraction. The speed that light can travel in water is less than the speed it can travel in air (because water is more dense). This difference in the speed of the light reaching the eye makes the stick look bent.

What are optical illusions?

Sometimes what we think we see is not what is really there. Our eyes are tricked by the behavior of the light reaching them. We call such tricks optical illusions. Shown here is a well-known one to try for yourself.

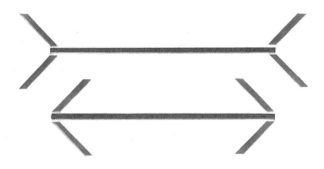

An optical illusion; although one seems longer, both these bars are the same length.

Do all animals see as well as humans?

Many animals have much better eyesight than humans. A hawk, for example, has eyes eight times as sharp as ours. But an elephant has poor eyesight. Like other vertebrates (animals with backbones), we have eyes with a single lens. Insects, such as bees, have compound eyes made up of thousands of lenses.

What is binocular vision?

Each of your two eyes presents your brain with a slightly different view of the world. The brain combines the two views into a single picture that has depth. Using only one eye, you see a view of the world that appears flat, like a photograph. Having binocular vision (two eyes in the front of the head) enables us to judge distance accurately. Binocular vision is particularly important for tree dwellers such as monkeys, and hunters such as owls and cats.

Animals that hunt have binocular vision to catch their prey.

Who first proved that white light is a mixture of colors?

Between 1665–66 Isaac Newton carried out experiments in a darkened room. He put a glass prism in a beam of sunlight streaming through a small hole in the wall and saw it split into the colors of the rainbow: red, orange, yellow, green, blue, indigo, and violet. When he placed a second prism in the colored beam, he saw the light rays bent back and become white again.

Isaac Newton discovered light to be a mixture of colors.

What makes the colors of the rainbow?

The rainbow is nature's spectrum. Falling drops of rain behave like tiny prisms. They break up white sunlight into the colors of the spectrum.

Why does the sky appear blue?

As white light from the Sun enters the Earth's atmosphere, it is reflected or "scattered" by millions of tiny dust particles and water droplets in the air. The light at the blue end of the spectrum is scattered most, and this is why the sky appears blue. Without the scattering effect of the atmosphere, the sky would look black—just as it does in outer space.

How can a spinning top demonstrate that Newton was right?

A simple experiment to show that light is a mixture of colors can be done with a spinning top made from a piece of cardboard. Paint the colors of the spectrum on the cardboard and watch it spin. The colors will mix before your eyes and the top will appear white.

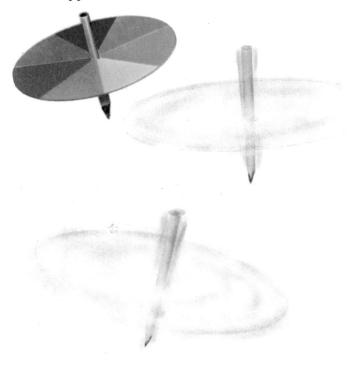

A top painted with the colors of the spectrum will seem white when spun.

What are the primary colors of light?

The primary colors of white light are red, green, and blue. Mixed together, they make white. The so-called secondary colors are magenta (blue-red), cyan (blue-green), and yellow.

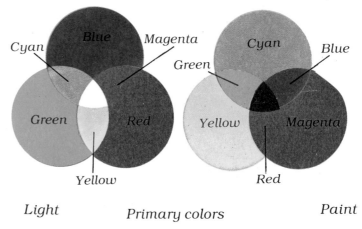

Light   Primary colors   Paint

Are paint colors the same as light colors?

Paints are made from pigments that absorb light just as other substances do. In paints, the primary colors are therefore not the same as in light. You cannot split white paint to make colors (as you can with light). Instead, you must add other colors to it. The three primary colors of paint are magenta (red), cyan (blue), and yellow. Mixed together, they make almost any color. You can make black by mixing them in the right combination, but you can never make white.

How do bees see flowers?

A bee can see ultraviolet light, which is invisible to the human eye. But a bee cannot see much red. A flower that looks white to us looks blue to a bee.

Why is grass green?

We see grass as green because of the way the grass reflects the light reaching it. The leaves absorb (take in) all the colors in light except green. The green is reflected. Under orange street lamps, grass looks black, because the grass absorbs the orange light and reflects hardly any light.

Mirrors and Lenses

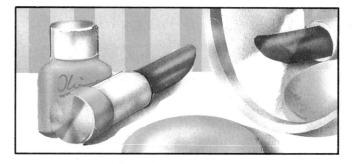

How are mirrors made?

The earliest mirrors were made of highly polished metal. The Romans used bronze mirrors. Making glass mirrors, by coating one side of the glass with silver to make it reflect light, was not perfected until the 1600s. The technique of "silvering" mirrors, by putting a film of silver on the back, was invented in 1835.

Why do mirrors reflect our images?

Everything reflects light, even the pages of this book. But most surfaces are rough, so the light is diffused, or spread in all directions. We can see the pages of this book from wherever we stand in the room. A mirror's smooth, shiny surface reflects light much more accurately as parallel rays and therefore gives a clear image.

Why is a mirror image the wrong way around?

Light always travels in straight lines so the mirror reflects light rays from your left side straight back to you on the left. So when you look at the mirror, your left side looks to be on your left. But if you were really looking at another person, his or her left side would be to your right.

Who first realized that mirrors reflect light at the same angle as the light reaches them?

More than 2,000 years ago a Greek named Hero of Alexandria experimented with mirrors. He noticed that the angle of a ray of light reaching the mirror was the same as the angle of the reflected light from the mirror. You can test this for yourself with a flashlight. Switch on the flashlight, and stand it to one side of a mirror. Note where you have to stand in order to see the reflection of the flashlight bulb in the mirror.

Convex mirrors magnify, concave mirrors reduce.

How does the curve of a mirror affect the reflection it gives?

A curved mirror distorts the image it reflects. Look at yourself in the bowl of a polished spoon. The bowl acts as a concave mirror. Your image will be upside down. Now turn the spoon over and look at yourself again. The back of the spoon acts as a convex mirror. Which way up is your reflection?

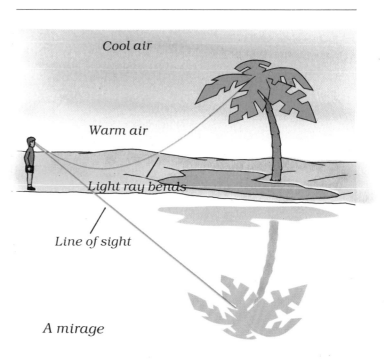

A mirage

Oddly curved mirrors such as those at fairgrounds reflect light in many different directions. The effects are sometimes strange, sometimes hilarious, and can make us look fat, thin, or even two-headed.

Why do funhouse mirrors make us laugh?

The funhouse mirrors in amusement arcades and fairgrounds make us laugh because they give us odd reflections of ourselves. They can make us look very short and fat, or very tall and thin. A funhouse mirror has a complicated curved surface which reflects light in many different directions.

What causes mirages?

On a hot day, the air near the ground heats up, expands, and becomes less dense. This causes light to bend in unusual ways, producing optical illusions known as mirages. A traveler in the desert may see what looks like water. It is actually the reflection of light from the sky bent by the layer of hot air close to the ground.

How can someone see beyond the horizon?

In certain conditions, when dense, cold air lies above the sea, it is possible to see a ship hidden beyond the horizon. Rays of light are bent by the cold air downward toward the Earth, giving an observer a view of a distant ship invisible in direct line of sight. If there is warm air above the cold layer, the rays may be bent again—and the ship will appear to be upside down!

Why are lenses different shapes?

Lenses are glass or plastic disks that bend light and can make objects look larger or smaller. A lens that is hollowed out (so that it is thinner in the middle than at the edges) is said to be *concave*. It spreads the light rays passing through it and makes objects look smaller. A lens that is rounded (thicker at the middle than at the edges) is *convex*. It concentrates, or narrows, the light and makes things look larger.

When did people first wear eyeglasses?

The Arabs knew of the magnifying glass about the year 1000. Soon after this, eyeglasses were being made. The first ones had two magnifying glass lenses fastened close together, instead of being placed over each eye as in modern eyeglasses. By 1300 there were eyeglasses to magnify (enlarge) objects close to the eyes, and by about 1430 glasses to help nearsighted people see distant objects more clearly were in use.

Who invented the telescope?

About 1600 a Dutch eyeglass maker named Hans Lippershey put two lenses together and looked through them at the weather vane on a distant church. He was startled to see how large the weather vane appeared. He had made the first telescope. He tried to patent his invention, but his application was rejected. Soon, though, telescopes were being made in Venice, Paris, and London. Many others tried to take the credit, one when he would have been only two years old.

Who said he had seen "flies as big as lambs"?

Galileo, the great astronomer

The great Italian scientist Galileo was very excited when he first heard of the telescope, in 1609. He made one himself and used it first for looking at near objects. He told a visitor that he had peered at flies through his telescope, and they appeared "as big as lambs." He discovered that flies were hairy and that they walked upside down by clinging to the ceiling with their feet.

When was the telescope first used to study the stars?

Galileo was a skillful instrument maker and his telescope was much more powerful than the first Dutch-made ones. He was also an astronomer, and he soon turned his new instrument toward the skies. He saw myriads of stars never seen before and also discovered four new "planets," which were in fact moons of Jupiter.

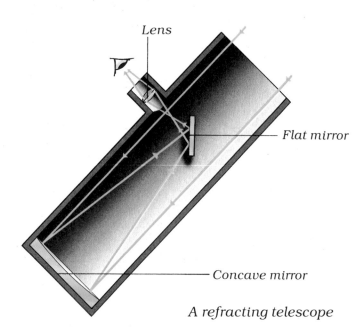

A refracting telescope

Lens

Flat mirror

Concave mirror

What are the largest telescopes in use today?

Most large modern optical telescopes are reflectors. The 5.5-yard telescope at Mount Palomar in California has a power of magnification of one million times. There is an even larger reflecting telescope in the Soviet Union. The world's biggest refracting telescope is at the Yerkes Observatory in Wisconsin and has a lens 3.35 feet across.

What is a radio telescope?

Telescopes can see only those objects in space that give off light. Distant objects give off other rays, such as radio waves. In the 1930s an American scientist named Karl Jansky picked up radio signals from far away in space. His discovery of "radio stars" led to the invention of the radio telescope, with which astronomers can study the most distant objects in the Universe.

Huge radio telescopes can detect emissions from stars and galaxies millions of light-years away.

How did Newton invent a better telescope?

Galileo's telescope was a *refracting* telescope. Because it relied on lenses, it had to be very long to magnify large amounts. Also, because colors were refracted to differing extents, the lenses produced distortion. In 1668 Isaac Newton built the first *reflecting* telescope. It had concave mirrors instead of lenses. It was only 6 inches long but had a magnification of 40 times, better than a refracting telescope 12 times as long. Mirrors reflect all colors equally, so the distortion problem was solved.

How does a periscope work?

A simple periscope can be made with two flat mirrors, set at an angle of 45°. Light is reflected from the top mirror down to the lower one. In this way, you can see over a wall or over the heads of taller people in a crowd. Submarines have periscopes so that the commander can observe the scene above water without bringing the submarine to the surface.

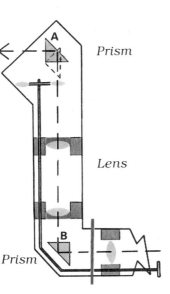

A simple periscope

Who invented the microscope?

The microscope was invented in the early 1600s, and there are several claimants for its invention, among them Zacharias Janssen of Holland. What is surprising is that lenses had been known and made for more than 300 years, but no one had thought of combining them to make either a microscope or a telescope.

Who saw a new world in a glass of pond water?

Antonie van Leeuwenhoek (1632–1723) of Holland used his own homemade single-lens microscope to study pond life. In 1674 he examined a glass of green swamp water and found in it "very many small animalcules." He had discovered bacteria. He was amazed to find that even a spoonful of water was alive with microscopic creatures, too small to be seen with the naked eye.

Antonie van Leeuwenhoek

What are the most powerful microscopes?

The best optical microscope cannot magnify an object more than 2,000 times. In 1924 a French scientist, Louis de Broglie, suggested that as atomic particles called electrons, like light, moved in waves, it should be possible to make an "electron microscope," more powerful than any optical instrument.

Electron micrograph of the head of a black fly

How does the electron microscope work?

The electron microscope was designed by Max Knoll and Ernst Ruska in Germany in 1932. The first one was crude but later improvements created a microscope that can magnify more than a million times. Electromagnetic fields are the microscope's "lenses." A hot wire filament sends a stream of electrons in a beam to hit the object to be examined. The denser areas of the object stop some electrons passing through. The rest travel on and hit a television screen or a photographic plate. The result is a "shadow picture" of the object.

Photography

Early photographers needed a huge amount of equipment.

How can light make pictures?

Light can cause changes in many substances. Colored curtains fade if left in a sunny window for a long time, for example. The word *photography* comes from Greek and means "drawing with light." The lens in a camera captures the light and records an image on the light-sensitive chemicals of the film inside.

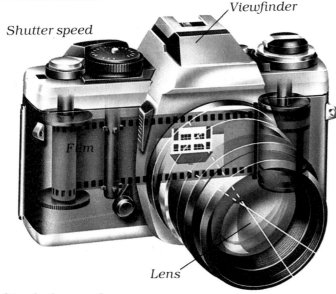

Single-lens reflex camera

Labels: *Shutter speed*, *Viewfinder*, *Film*, *Lens*

What was a camera obscura?

The camera obscura was a device used by artists. It was a darkened room with a pin hole in one wall. Light passing through the pin hole produced an inverted image of the scene outside on the opposite wall. The artist traced over the image to produce an accurate outline for his finished painting or drawing.

When was the first photograph taken?

The earliest known photograph was taken by the French scientist Joseph Niépce in 1826. It was made on an asphalt-coated pewter plate, and shows a view from a window. The exposure took eight hours.

How was "instant" photography made possible?

In 1947 Edwin Land, an American, invented the Polaroid camera. In his camera, the film was developed automatically by chemicals inside, instead of having to be developed and printed in a dark room. It was the first "instant" camera.

Why was photography not invented earlier?

Although the camera obscura was known from the Middle Ages, no one managed to make a camera that could fix an image until the early 1800s. The problem was in getting the right chemicals. In the end the solution was to spread thin layers of light-sensitive silver salts onto glass plates.

Who were the pioneers of photography?

In the 1830s and 1840s two photographic processes were developed. They were the daguerreotype of the Frenchman L. J. M. Daguerre and the calotype of the Englishman W. H. Fox Talbot. The daguerreotype used a silver-copper plate instead of glass. It took a minute to expose the plate, so the sitter in a portrait had to remain motionless for that time. Fox Talbot found a way of making positive paper prints from a negative. In 1888 the American George Eastman invented the Kodak camera, which used roll film instead of cumbersome plates.

When were color photographs first taken?

Photographers began experimenting with color film as early as 1861, but it did not come into commercial use until the late 1930s.

Radiation

Are there more rays that we cannot see?

In the 1870s James Clerk Maxwell predicted other forms of radiation beyond the visible spectrum—in other words, ones we cannot see. For example, if a thermometer is used to measure the light in the spectrum, it will detect a rise in temperature at the red end. Beyond the red end of the visible spectrum are heat rays, called infrared rays, and it is their presence that causes the temperature rise.

The electromagnetic spectrum

Gamma rays   X-rays   Ultra-violet   Infra-red   Micro-waves   Radio waves

What is the electromagnetic spectrum?

The electromagnetic spectrum is a band of radiation of which light is just one part. The rays travel through space in waves of varying lengths. We can see light rays. But other parts of the spectrum are invisible to the eye. At the red end of the visible light spectrum are infrared, microwaves, radar, television, and radio waves. At the other (violet) end of the spectrum are ultraviolet, X-rays, gamma rays, and cosmic rays.

What causes a hot poker to glow white-hot?

An iron poker left in a glowing fire will heat up and start to glow. First it glows red, then yellow, and finally white. The more energy an object has, the greater the amount of radiation it gives off. As the poker heats up, it receives more energy. The light that it gives off moves through the spectrum toward blue. When the metal is hot enough to glow with all the colors, it looks white.

How can a spectrum tell us about the stars?

Astronomers can detect dark lines in the spectrum of the Sun and of other stars. This is because certain elements absorb certain wavelengths as light passes through the Sun's atmosphere. Each element makes a recognizable pattern of lines. So by studying the spectrum, astronomers can tell what the Sun and other stars are made of.

What is meant by the frequency of a wave?

The frequency of a wave is its rate of vibration. The length of a wave is the distance between its top, or crest, and the top of the next wave. Frequency is the number of waves that pass a fixed point every second. Light travels very fast and has a very high frequency.

What are short and long waves?

All electromagnetic radiation travels at the same speed, that of light. But each type has a different wavelength. Radio waves may be thousands of yards long. Cosmic rays are very short, less than one hundred-million-millionth of a yard.

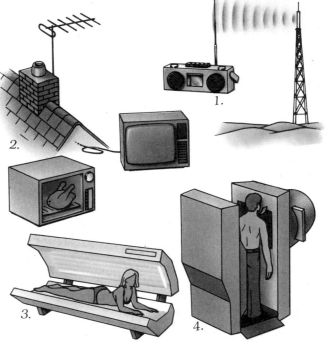

1. Radio and TV 2. Microwave 3. Tanning machine 4. X-ray machine

What kind of rays protect us from being ill?

The ultraviolet rays in sunlight are vital to health. Our bodies need this radiation to make vitamin D, which prevents a disease called rickets.

What causes sunburn?

Ultraviolet rays penetrate only a little way into our skin. While the rays enable the skin cells to make vitamin D, they also do damage to the outer layer of skin. The body reacts by making more of the brown pigment called melanin. This keeps the ultraviolet rays from penetrating too far. The Earth's atmosphere shields us from too much exposure to the harmful effects of ultraviolet rays.

What are infrared rays?

We feel infrared rays when we sit in front of a radiator fire and feel the "radiant" heat from its bars. More than half of the Sun's energy comes to us in the form of infrared rays.

What can infrared photography show up?

Infrared photography from space satellites can detect tiny temperature changes on Earth. They can be used to reveal diseased crops in fields and to track warm and cold water currents in the oceans.

Infrared photograph

Tanned skin protects against the Sun's harmful rays, but too much sun will damage your skin.

What is a "cool spot"?

Wherever the Sun casts a shadow, there is a cool spot, a patch of ground which remains cooler than its surroundings after the shadow has gone. The infrared camera of a spy satellite in space can detect the cool spot left by a tank or a missile transporter after the vehicle has moved away.

What causes fluorescence?

When ultraviolet rays strike some substances, the atoms of the substance absorb the rays and then give off rays with a longer wavelength. This is fluorescence. Fluorescent light can be seen with the naked eye, though ultraviolet light cannot.

Who discovered X-rays?

The German scientist Wilhelm Roentgen discovered X-rays by accident in 1895. He was experimenting with a cathode ray tube and noticed that crystals in the same room glowed when the tube was switched on. Even when he moved the crystals to the next room, they still glowed. Roentgen realized that invisible rays were causing the glow, rays that could even penetrate solid walls. He called them X-rays (X=unknown). In some countries X-rays are known as Roentgen rays.

How do X-rays give doctors pictures of the insides of our bodies?

If a human body is placed between an X-ray source and a photographic film or fluorescent screen, the X-rays produce a shadow picture of the inside of the body. X-rays are absorbed more by solid matter, such as bones, than by flesh.

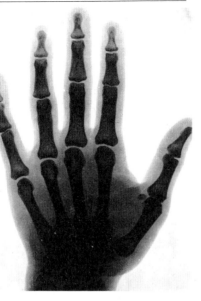

An X-ray of the human hand

So the bones, and any breaks in them, are clearly seen. An object opaque to X-rays, such as a swallowed button, is also clearly visible on the X-ray photographs.

What are microwaves?

Microwaves lie beyond infrared waves in the spectrum. They have very short wavelengths and are used by astronomers to study distant bodies in space. They are also used in radar. Microwave beams are used to transmit TV pictures around the world.

How does a microwave oven work?

In a microwave oven, a device called a magnetron changes electrical energy into microwaves. The microwaves reflect off all the surfaces of the inside of the oven. They pass through food containers but are absorbed by any food or liquid in them. By vibrating the molecules in the food, they produce heat which cooks the food more rapidly than in a conventional oven.

RAdio **D**etection **A**nd **R**anging (Radar)

Display

How was radar invented?

Radar was invented in the 1930s. Robert Watson-Watt, a Scottish scientist, was asked to investigate reports that Germany was working on a "death ray," using radio beams. There was no such ray. But Watson-Watt's research provided an answer to the problem of detecting ships and aircraft. Called radiolocation, it worked by transmitting a radio beam from the ground. Any object crossing the beam (such as an aircraft) produced an "echo," and this could be received on the ground and used to plot the height and position of the aircraft.

When was radar first used in war?

By 1936 a number of radar stations had been set up secretly in Britain. These stations played a key role in the Battle of Britain during World War II. Radar gave early warning of approaching bombers and so helped the Royal Air Force to fight off the German air raids.

How can X-rays reveal an art forgery?

Art experts use X-ray photographs to examine paintings and sculptures. Sometimes the X-ray reveals a hidden picture, painted over by the artist, or alterations made by someone else. X-rays can also show whether a piece of sculpture or metalwork is really as old as is claimed. Sometimes the X-rays reveal tell-tale signs that it is a modern forgery.

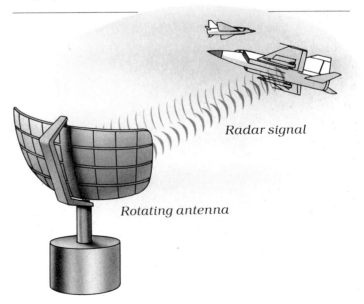

Radar signal

Rotating antenna

Lasers and Holograms

What is the difference between laser light and ordinary light?

A laser produces a very powerful beam of light, so powerful it can burn a hole through metal. Unlike the beam from a flashlight, a laser beam spreads hardly at all. Laser light contains light of only one color, unlike sunlight which is a mixture of colors. Laser light is said to be *coherent*; its waves are all exactly alike, and all in "step."

How did the laser get its name?

The first laser was made in 1960 by an American scientist named Theodore H. Maiman. Its name comes from a set of initials standing for **L**ight **A**mplification by **S**timulated **E**mission of **R**adiation.

What are the three main parts of a laser?

A laser has three main parts. They are 1) the medium, the material that produces the beam (such as a ruby crystal or a gas); 2) the power source that energizes the medium; 3) the resonator to make the beam more powerful (usually mirrors that reflect the light backward and forward to build up its strength).

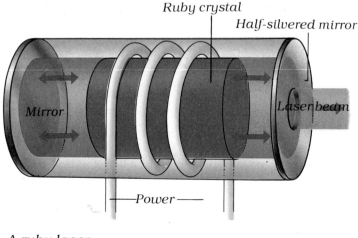

Ruby crystal

Half-silvered mirror

Mirror

Laser beam

Power

A ruby laser

Why are lasers used in eye surgery?

Lasers are used by doctors to perform delicate surgery, such as reattaching a damaged retina in the eye. The laser treatment is painless and the patient remains conscious during the operation. He or she must be kept still while the laser is at work, but because the laser pulses are so rapid (each one lasts only a thousandth of a second) the eye does not have time to see them and so there is no fear of the patient blinking.

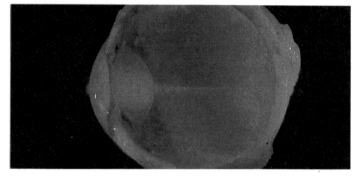

A laser being used to repair a displaced retina.

How do surveyors and builders use lasers?

A laser can be used by a surveyor as an infinitely tall "ranging pole," from which to take bearings and measurements. The laser beam is fired vertically into the sky and provides an easily detected fixed point for other surveyors, even if hills and forests are in the way. Builders of skyscrapers use laser beams like plumb lines to check that the building is vertical. Unlike an ordinary plumb line (which would not be long enough in any case), a laser beam cannot be blown sideways by the wind.

How were lasers used to measure the distance from the Earth to the Moon?

Because the laser beam is so straight and narrow, it makes an excellent measuring instrument for astronomers. The Apollo astronauts who landed on the Moon in 1969 left behind a laser reflector. A laser beam was fired from Earth to hit the reflector, and the beam bounced back to Earth. The calculation of the time it took the laser beam to travel there and back produced a figure for the distance between the Earth and Moon accurate to within 6 inches.

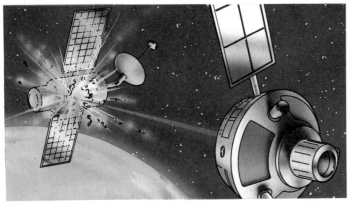

A thing of the future: a space laser destroying an enemy satellite.

Can lasers be used as weapons?

Lasers are used by soldiers as target finders. The laser beam is fired at the target (such as a tank) and a guided missile flies along the beam, following it until it hits the target. Experiments are being made with lasers as space weapons, for destroying satellites and ballistic missiles. The "light sabers" used in the *Star Wars* films remain in the world of future fantasy.

What is a 3-D picture?

When you look at an ordinary photograph, the objects in it have no depth. A photograph of the front of a car, for example, looks the same from any angle. No matter where you stand, you can never see the side of the car. A 3-D, or three-dimensional, picture makes an object appear to have depth. If you move to one side, you see a different view of the object. In the example of the car, you would be able to see the side of the car. This effect can be created in a special kind of image called a *hologram.*

What is a hologram?

The Greek word *holos* means "whole." A hologram is a "whole picture." A hologram is made by illuminating an object with laser light. The three-dimensional picture is viewed by shining a laser of the same color or wavelength through the hologram. The principle of the hologram was worked out by the Hungarian-born physicist Dennis Gabor in 1948, but making holograms was not possible before the invention of the laser.

How are holograms made?

Holograms are made by splitting the light from a laser into two beams. One beam, the object beam, is reflected from a mirror through a lens onto the object (say, a chair), then back to the holographic plate. The other beam, the reference beam, is reflected through another mirror and lens and spreads out over the holographic plate. Where the two beams meet, an "interference pattern" is formed. This pattern contains the picture information needed to create a 3-D image of the chair when the plate is exposed to the same kind of laser light again.

Hologram

How can a whole picture library be stored in a tiny crystal?

Holograms can be used to store lots of pictures in a very small space. Using a laser, a hologram picture is produced inside a crystal of a substance called lithium niobate. The crystal is moved very slightly and a second picture is added, and so on, until hundreds of pictures are stored inside. The pictures can be looked at in turn by shining a laser beam into the crystal at the same precise angle as when each hologram was made.

How can light be used to send telephone calls?

In a telephone, sounds are changed into electrical signals and sent through wires. In 1966 scientists succeeded in using lasers to carry telephone calls, by changing the electrical signals into light-pulses. Instead of wires, they used optical fibers—very long, thin glass rods. A single optical fiber can carry as many as 2,000 telephone conversations and yet weighs much less than copper wire. The light-pulses travel inside the glass rods, kept in by the mirror-like inside wall of the fiber. At the end of the optical-fiber cable the pulses are changed back into sounds.

Sound

What causes sound?

Sounds can be very different—the roar of a jet engine, the music of an orchestra, the song of a bird—but all sounds are made in a similar way. When an object vibrates (moves backward and forward), it produces sound.

How does sound travel?

Sound is a form of energy. Like light, it travels in waves. But sound needs something to travel through. Sound can travel through any substance that has molecules able to move, so it cannot travel in a vacuum such as outer space.

How fast does sound travel?

Sound travels far more slowly than light. If you were to witness a powerful explosion many miles away, your eyes would see the flash of the explosion before your ears heard the noise. Sound travels through air at around 1,100 feet a second. The colder the air, the slower sound travels.

Can you hear under water?

Sounds travel faster through water than through air, at about 1,300 feet a second. Sound travels even faster through steel—at around 19,700 feet a second. The reason is that liquids (water) and solids (steel) are more elastic than gases (such as air). Their molecules pass on energy more easily and pass on the sound waves more quickly.

Why is the Moon a silent world?

The Moon has no air, so no sound can travel across its surface. The astronauts who landed on the Moon could talk to one another by radio. But there were no other sounds to be heard, not even when they hit a piece of rock with a hammer. Sound cannot travel through the airless vacuum of outer space.

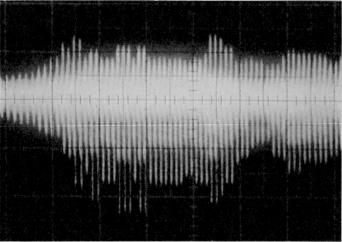

A display showing the sound vibrations in the sentence "Where are you?"

Sounds are caused by vibration.

Why are concert halls and recording studios soundproofed?

Hard surfaces reflect sound, and soft surfaces absorb sound. The study of controlling sounds is known as *acoustics*, and it is important when designing buildings in which people want to hear some sounds but keep out others. Concert halls and recording studios must be sealed to keep out unwanted sounds such as traffic noise. Unwanted sounds will find their way through the floors and walls, unless the hall or studio is soundproofed with soft, sound-absorbing materials.

What causes an echo?

Have you ever stood inside an old cathedral and heard your voice echoing from the thick, stone walls? The same thing happens inside a cave, or where there are cliffs or high walls. The echo is caused by the sound waves bouncing off the hard wall. The sound is reflected back to your ear and you hear an echo of your voice.

Sonar picture of a crashed World War II bomber.

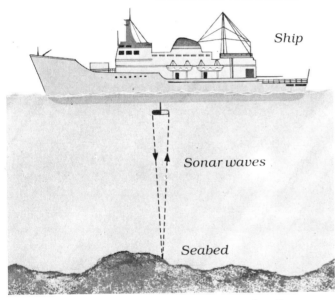

Ship

Sonar waves

Seabed

Ships use sonar to measure water depth.

How are echoes used to chart the seabed?

Ships use echo sounders, devices that send out pulses of sound, to tell how deep the water is. The sound waves travel down to the seabed and are reflected back to the ship. Measuring the time this takes, and knowing how fast sound travels in water, enables the depth of water to be worked out. This technique is known as *sonar*, which is short for "**SO**und **NA**vigation and **R**anging."

Is there really a sound barrier?

Before the late 1940s no aircraft had flown faster than sound. Test pilots had difficulty in controlling propeller-driven planes which could approach the speed of sound only in a dive and people wondered if there was a mysterious "sound barrier." But the invention of jet planes proved this idea was wrong. Jets flew faster than sound without being shaken apart and without harm to their pilots. Today *Concorde* regularly carries passengers across the Atlantic at twice the speed of sound.

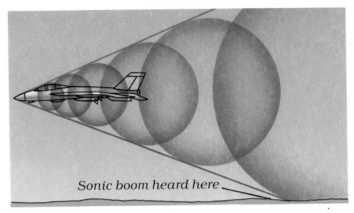

Sonic boom heard here

Shock waves produced by supersonic aircraft.

Why does a supersonic aircraft make a sonic boom when it flies overhead?

An aircraft flying below the speed of sound flies inside a pattern of pressure waves caused by its movement through the air. As it approaches the speed of sound, the plane catches up with the pressure waves and above the speed of sound the plane leaves them behind. A cone-shaped shock wave is formed and as this shock wave passes, people on the ground hear a noise called the sonic boom.

What is the difference between loudness and pitch?

The loudness of a sound depends on the distance moved by the vibrating object producing the sound. The greater its movement, the louder the sound. Loudness is measured in *decibels*. The pitch is how high or low a sound is and depends on the speed of the vibrations. The number of vibrations per second is a sound's frequency, and this is measured in *hertz* (Hz).

Are there sounds we cannot hear?

Human ears are most sensitive to sounds at around 2,000 hertz (*see previous question*). The lowest sound we can hear is about 16 Hz and the highest is about 20,000 Hz. Dogs can hear higher-pitched sounds. Some dog owners use whistles that make a sound too high for them to hear, but which is heard perfectly well by their pet.

How do bats use ultrasound?

Ultrasound is sound too high-pitched for humans to hear. Bats can hear and produce sounds up to 100,000 Hz in frequency. They use ultrasound as an echo-sounding device for navigation and hunting. The bat gives out very high-pitched squeaks and uses its large ears to pick up the echoes. The echoes tell the bat the exact location of prey (such as a moth) or of an obstacle (such as a tree or a cave wall). The bat's sonar is so good that it can fly unerringly in the dark, even in a room full of obstacles.

Ultrasound scan of an unborn baby

How do doctors examine unborn babies with the help of sound waves?

Ultrasonic waves penetrate flesh and other soft body parts, just like X-rays, and they can be used to produce pictures of the inside of the body. Because the sound waves have no harmful effects, doctors use ultrasonic scanners to examine pregnant women. The scan shows if the unborn baby in the womb is healthy and growing properly.

How powerful is sound?

Loud noises can cause physical pain and damage the hearing. In humans, any noise louder than 140 decibels (louder than a jet engine) can cause pain. High-powered ultrasound can be concentrated, like a laser beam, and can drill holes or weld metal together.

What is resonance?

If you sing into an open piano, with the loud pedal pressed down, you will get a surprise. The piano will sing back to you. What happens is that your voice sets up vibrations in the piano strings. This effect is called resonance. The violin and acoustic guitar are musical instruments which make use of resonance. Their bodies vibrate with the strings, giving an amplified and richer sound.

When were sounds first recorded?

The first sound recording was made by the American inventor Thomas Alva Edison in 1877 on a machine he called the phonograph. Sounds were picked up by a vibrating membrane, and the vibrations made a needle cut spiral grooves on a cylinder covered with tinfoil. When a second needle was moved along the grooves, the sounds were reproduced by means of another vibrating membrane and amplified through a horn.

Drum

Hearing tube

Edison's phonograph, the first record player

Who made the first recording disks?

In 1887 Emile Berliner made recordings on flat disks, rather than on cylinders. He called his recording machine a gramophone.

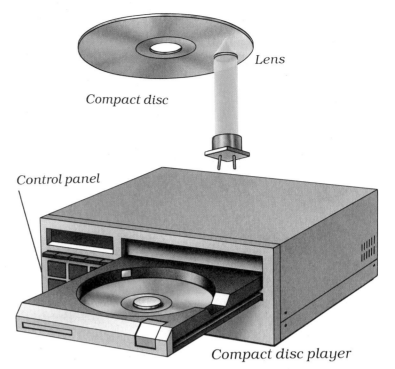

Compact disc

Lens

Control panel

Compact disc player

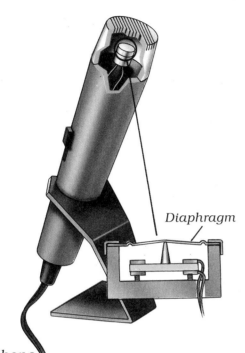

Diaphragm

A microphone

How does a microphone work?

A microphone changes sound waves into electric current which can be fed along a wire. The simplest type is the telephone microphone which has a diaphragm, or vibrating membrane, that transmits sound waves to carbon granules. As the granules are moved by the incoming sounds, they in turn cause changes in an electrical current. The electrical signals travel through wires, and are turned back into sounds at the receiver.

When was recording tape first used?

The first experiments with sound recording on tape were made in 1898 by the Danish inventor Valdemar Poulsen, using magnetized metal wire. In the 1930s paper tapes were developed and reel-to-reel tape recorders appeared in the 1940s. Today's cassette players use plastic tape coated with magnetic material.

What is digital recording?

In most recording systems, the electrical signals are stored as a continuous wave pattern. These build up a replica or *analog* of the original sounds. In digital recording, the sound waves are converted into electrical pulses which are coded as a series of numbers (digits) in binary form. To replay the sound, the signals are decoded back into analog form (although completely digital systems are being developed). Digital recordings give more accurate reproduction because they store much more information about the sounds being recorded. Nowadays digital recordings have to be stored on compact discs instead of on ordinary tapes, but digital tape is available.

How can 100-year-old records be made to sound as if they were made yesterday?

Old records sound scratchy because the recording methods of the past were primitive. Also, they are fragile, easily cracked or broken. A computerized system known as digital signal processing can re-record old records. Where there are gaps or hisses in the record, the computer fills them in, imitating the sounds of music or singing elsewhere on the record. In this way almost-perfect tape copies of old and historic recordings can be made. So we can hear what famous singers from the past, such as Enrico Caruso, really sounded like.

ENERGY AND MOTION

What is energy?

Energy is the ability to do work. When you walk upstairs, your body is working, and uses energy. The spring inside a clockwork motor provides the energy to drive the mechanism. A flashlight battery provides the energy needed to light up the bulb. The Sun's energy enables plants to grow. In fact, all living things depend on the Sun for their energy. Energy can neither be created nor destroyed, it can only be changed into a different form, for example, the potential energy of a drawn bow into the kinetic energy of a flying arrow.

What is work?

To most people, "work" means many things: sitting in an office, assembling components in a factory, studying in school, mowing the lawn, doing the laundry, and so on. To a scientist, work is what happens when energy produces a force that moves or changes an object. The unit used to measure work is called the *joule*, and is named after the British physicist James Prescott Joule, who lived between 1818 and 1889.

Where does energy come from?

Energy comes from matter. Everything in the Universe is made up of matter, so in some form energy is found everywhere. Even the tiniest atomic particles can be changed into energy. Matter can be changed into energy and energy can be changed into matter. Neither can be destroyed.

The stretched bow has potential energy; the flying arrow has kinetic energy.

Can energy change its form?

When you lift a hammer to hit a nail, the raised hammer gains potential energy. As the hammer hits the nail that energy is made to work. The nail is driven into the wood. Potential, or stored, energy has been changed to kinetic energy, or energy of motion. Similarly, heat energy can be changed into electrical energy; electrical energy can become radiant energy (such as light); and chemical energy can become mechanical energy.

How many forms of energy are there?

Energy that is stored up is called *potential* energy. Water stored behind a dam, an archer's bow drawn and ready to fire: both these are examples of potential energy. Falling water and an arrow shot from a bow each have *kinetic* energy. Potential and kinetic energy are both forms of mechanical energy. There are other kinds of energy too: thermal, or heat, energy, chemical energy, nuclear energy, and radiant energy.

What is the greatest source of energy known on the Earth?

Nuclear energy, or energy from the atom, is the greatest energy source we know on Earth. When the nucleus of an atom splits, far more energy is released at one time than from any other source of energy. A small amount of matter (a lump of uranium, for example) becomes a huge amount of energy.

Natural gas burning off from a pipeline

What are fossil fuels?

Much of the energy we use at home and at work comes from the burning of so-called fossil fuels such as coal, oil, and gas. These fuels were formed millions of years ago from the remains of plants and animals.

Why do people talk of an "energy crisis"?

There are only limited stocks of fossil fuels. Once the world's coal, oil, and gas reserves have been used up, we shall have to turn to other sources of energy. Already, scientists are examining alternatives, such as wind and wave power, solar power (using sunlight), and safe nuclear power. To make our remaining fossil fuels last as long as possible, it is important not to waste energy.

Why do things become hot?

Heat is the transfer of energy from one substance to another. If you rub a piece of cloth with your hand, the cloth will begin to feel warmer. The rubbing has produced heat as a result of friction.

What is the coldest anything can be?

When a substance is warmed, its molecules move around faster. When it is cooled, they move more slowly. The coldest that anything can get is when its molecules stop moving. This is at a temperature of minus 459.6 degrees Fahrenheit ($-459.6°F$), or "absolute zero." Scientists have produced temperatures within a fraction of absolute zero, but have not yet achieved zero itself.

Liquid helium "refrigerator"

What can make a jug of liquid empty itself?

When they are supercooled, substances may behave very oddly. Some become *superconductors*, allowing electricity to flow through them very easily. Others become "superfluids," slipping through the narrowest crack and even climbing out of a container. If liquid helium (at a temperature below -456 degrees Fahrenheit) is put into a jug, it will overflow, even though the jug is only half full.

Why does a metal saucepan handle get hot?

Substances that carry heat well are called good conductors of heat. Metals are the best conductors. A metal saucepan cooks well because it allows heat from the cooker to pass into the food inside. But the pan itself also becomes very hot, and so will the handle unless it is covered with a material that does not conduct heat so well.

Why do railway tracks get longer in summer?

The rails of railway track have small gaps at their joints. This seems odd, for surely the trains would run more smoothly without the joints. There is a good reason, however. Metals expand (get bigger) when hot. So in hot weather, the railway track gets slightly longer. Without the small gap, the force of the rails pushing together would make the track buckle and twist.

What makes the currents of water inside an electric teapot?

When you fill a teapot with cold water and switch it on, you will quickly see currents beginning to move in the water around the heating element. The heat from the element warms the water closest to it. Warm water rises, because when a liquid is heated it expands and becomes lighter. As the warm water rises, cold water moves to take its place and is heated in its turn. Such currents are called *convection* currents.

Anders Celsius

How can heat travel?

Heat travels in several ways. The heat you feel when you hold a saucepan handle is carried by *conduction*. The heat energy inside an electric teapot is carried by convection. A radiator with a shiny reflector sends out heat waves by *radiation*.

Who invented the Celsius scale for measuring temperature?

The earliest scale for measuring temperature was invented by a Dutchman named Gabriel Fahrenheit in the early 1700s. This scale, named after him, has the freezing point of water at 32 degrees and the boiling point at 212 degrees. In 1742 a Swede named Anders Celsius suggested a scale in which the freezing point of water would be fixed as 0 degrees. In the Centigrade or Celsius scale the boiling point of water is 100 degrees. The symbol ° is used for degrees. We usually write 30 degrees Celsius as 30°C, and so on.

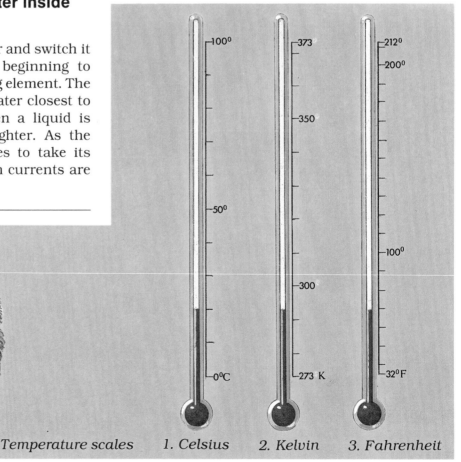

Temperature scales 1. Celsius 2. Kelvin 3. Fahrenheit

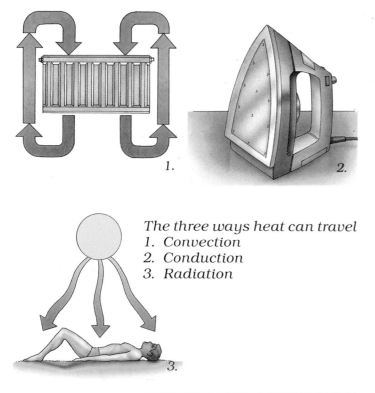

The three ways heat can travel
1. *Convection*
2. *Conduction*
3. *Radiation*

Huge icebergs conceal 90% of their bulk under water.

What is the Kelvin scale?

Scientists use the Kelvin scale, which starts at absolute zero (or −459.69°F). In this scale, absolute zero is 0K, water freezes at 273.16K, and water boils at 373.16K. The scale is named after the British scientist Lord Kelvin, who suggested it in 1848.

How hot and cold can things be?

The centers of stars are enormously hot, up to 20 million degrees Kelvin (K). The surface of our Sun is around 6,000K. In outer space it is very cold and the temperature can approach absolute zero (0K).

Why can ducks swim happily in freezing water?

The feathers of birds, such as ducks, keep them warm by trapping layers of air next to the skin. Air is a poor conductor of heat, so the layers of air act as an insulating "cold barrier." Thanks to its insulation, a duck keeps warm even in cold water. A double-glazed window does the same job in a building.

Why does an iceberg float?

Unlike most liquids, water expands (gets bigger) when it freezes and becomes less dense as a result. An ice cube will therefore float in a glass of water and not sink. This fact explains why huge icebergs float and also why rivers do not freeze solid in winter. Ice forms as a floating layer on top, and this layer stops further freezing beneath. If the ice sank to the bottom, the river would quickly freeze solid.

How does a thermometer work?

A thermometer is an instrument for measuring temperature. A narrow tube is filled with liquid (usually mercury or alcohol). As the temperature rises, the liquid inside the tube expands and is forced up the tube. As the temperature falls, the liquid contracts and sinks back down the tube. The Italian scientist Galileo invented a primitive thermometer in 1592.

Simple Machines

What are the oldest known machines?

A machine is a device for doing work, and the oldest known machines are the simplest, such as the wedge, the lever, and the inclined plane. These were used by Stone Age people 100,000 years ago. Their inventors are unknown. The wheel was a later discovery and was not in common use until about 5,000 years ago.

How does a lever work?

The lever is a simple machine that moves objects. The commonest kind is called a *first-class* lever. The object to be moved is known as the *load*, and the force needed to move it is called the *effort*. The lever needs a pivot, or *fulcrum*. Using a branch as a lever and resting it on a small rock (the fulcrum), it is possible to lift a much heavier weight. When Stone Age people discovered this, they had invented one of mankind's basic machines: the lever.

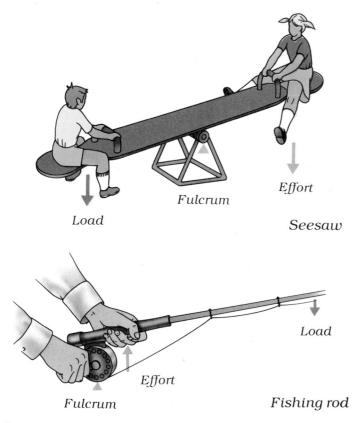

Seesaw

Load — *Fulcrum* — *Effort*

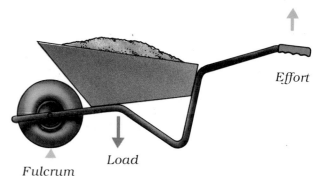

Wheelbarrow

Effort — *Load* — *Fulcrum*

How can a wheelbarrow be a lever?

The wheelbarrow is an example of a *second-class* lever. On a first-class or simple lever, the fulcrum is between the load and the effort. (Think of a seesaw and you will get the idea.) Where is the fulcrum on a wheelbarrow? (*Look at the picture to see if you were correct.*)

An Egyptian shadoof used for irrigation.

How was a lever used to irrigate fields?

In ancient Egypt farmers used a machine called the shadoof to raise water from the river and empty it into ditches to water their crops. The shadoof works on the same principle as a simple lever. This ancient machine has remained in use until modern times.

What kind of lever is a fishing rod?

A fishing rod is an example of a third kind of lever. The effort (the angler's pulling hand) is applied between the fulcrum (the handle of the rod) and the load (the fish on the end of the line).

Fishing rod

Fulcrum — *Effort* — *Load*

Who claimed he could move the Earth with a lever?

The Greek scientist Archimedes, who lived more than 2,000 years ago, understood an important law or principle concerning levers. The law is that the effort (E) needed to lift the load (L) multiplied by the distance moved by the effort (dE) is equal to the weight of the load (L) multiplied by the distance the load moves (dL). As a mathematical equation, this can be written as:

$$E \times dE = L \times dL$$

If the effort moves through a large distance, a much heavier weight can be moved through a shorter distance. Realizing this, Archimedes is supposed to have said, "Give me a place to stand and I will move the Earth."

How were the Pyramids built?

The pyramids of ancient Egypt are huge structures, built more than 4,000 years ago. Great blocks of stone were used, each stone being hauled into place by hundreds of slaves. To raise the heavy stones, a ramp of earth was made and the stones were dragged up the ramp on wooden rollers. The ramp was a machine called an *inclined plane*. Look at a builder filling a wheelbarrow with rubbish. When he walks up a plank to empty his barrow, he is using an inclined plane, just as the ancient Egyptians did.

What kind of wedge tills the soil?

The wedge is another simple machine. Stone Age people used hand axes to split wood and shape flint into tools. The hand ax was wedge-shaped. Later, farmers adapted the wedge to break up the soil and the plow was invented.

Why is a screw a kind of inclined plane?

The screw thread is actually an inclined plane that goes around and around in a spiral. When you turn a nut on a bolt, the nut travels along the thread. It is "climbing" the spiral of the twisted inclined plane.

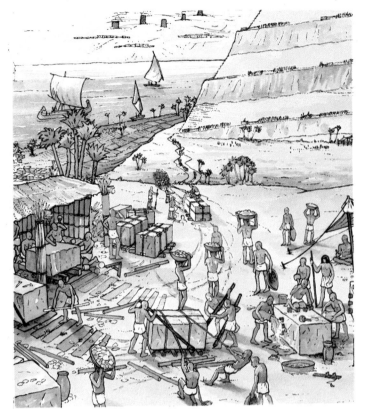

The Egyptians used rollers to move the huge stones when building the pyramids.

How can a wrench be a wheel?

A wrench is an example of a wheel and axle. The effort (through the handle) moves in a greater radius than the force produced (on the nut). The greater distance moved by the handle produces a greater force on the nut; so a long-handled wrench exerts greater force than a short one.

Why is it easy to lift a car using a jack?

Only a superstrong person can lift a car off the ground unaided. But using a screw jack, almost anyone can raise a car off the ground sufficiently to change a tire. The jack has a screw turned by a handle. The handle travels a long distance to raise the car a very short distance, and this gives the jack a great *mechanical advantage*. If by moving the jack handle through a distance of 4 inches, the car is raised just 0.4 inch, the jack is said to have a mechanical advantage of 100. By applying a force of 20 pounds to the jack handle, a person using such a jack could in principle lift a weight of 2,000 pounds (a ton).

How do more pulleys make less work?

A pulley is a useful machine for changing the direction of a force. For example, by pulling downward on a rope running over a pulley wheel, you can lift a load upward. The more pulleys there are, with one continuous rope running through them, the greater the mechanical advantage and so the greater the load that can be lifted with the same effort.

Roman crane with a human treadmill

When were building cranes first used?

The Romans introduced the crane, a machine for lifting loads using the principle of the pulley. Their cranes were worked by treadmills. Slaves trudging inside the treadmill produced the effort needed to lift the load of building stone.

Who used a screw to pump water?

Archimedes was once asked to devise a method of pumping water from the hold of a ship. He came up with the idea of a screw, turned by a handle inside a wooden cylinder. As the handle was turned, the screw raised water from the ship's hold. It was a much easier and quicker method than lowering buckets on the end of a rope.

How did a bored boy improve the steam engine?

Early steam engines were so slow that tending them must have been tedious. Two people were needed. One looked after the fire beneath the boiler, the other (usually a boy) opened and closed the stop valves. These controlled the flow of steam into the cylinder and of the cold water needed to condense it. Bored with his task, an engine tender named Humphrey Potter made an arrangement of cords attached to the beam of his engine, so that the stop valves opened and shut automatically. By doing so he also doubled the speed at which the engine worked.

How do gears work?

A gear is a wheel with teeth along its rim. The teeth fit, or mesh, with teeth on other wheels. As one wheel turns, so do the others. Gear wheels can be used to change the direction of a movement, and also to increase the speed and power of a machine. A big wheel with 40 teeth, for example, will turn at a quarter the speed of a wheel with ten teeth, if they are connected. But it will have four times as much power. A car in low gear moves slowly, but has more power for starting and going uphill. In high gear, it moves much faster but has less power.

Why did the pennyfarthing bicycle have such a huge front wheel?

A bicycle has gears to make pedaling less hard work. In low gear, one turn of the pedals produces a smaller turn of the wheels than it does in high gear. Selecting low gear makes it easier when cycling uphill. The pennyfarthing bicycle of the 1800s had no gears. Instead it had a very large front wheel. One turn of the pedals produced a large movement of the wheel, and this meant the pennyfarthing could travel faster than other gearless bikes of the day.

Force and Motion

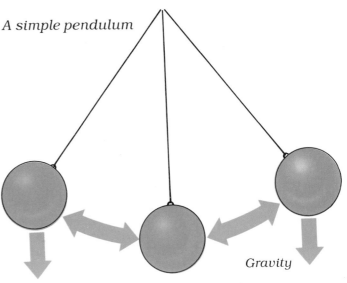

A simple pendulum

Gravity

What is inertia?

To start an object moving, a force is needed. When you kick a ball, the ball begins to move. It keeps moving until some other force stops it. The ball has inertia. It rolls on until stopped by another force (your foot perhaps, or a wall, or the friction of the ground). All moving objects have inertia; they try to keep moving until a force opposes them.

Inertia keeps bodies moving unless opposed—in this case by a truck.

Why do people fall forward when a bus stops suddenly?

Have you ever been standing on a bus when it pulled up suddenly? People are thrown forward because of the inertia affecting their bodies. Of course Isaac Newton, the great English scientist, never stood on a bus, but he understood about inertia. In his first law of motion (1687) Newton stated that every object remains in motion, or stays motionless, unless acted on by another force.

Why does a pendulum swing?

You can make a simple pendulum by fastening a weight to the end of a length of cord. Hold the cord so that the weight hangs vertically. When you give the pendulum a push, it swings away from you. The force of your push gives it motion. When it reaches the lowest point of its swing, the pendulum does not stop but swings on, this time upward. Inertia keeps it going until a stronger force (gravity) halts its motion and the pendulum swings back down toward the vertical again.

How does a pile driver work?

A pile driver, used on construction sites, is a huge hammer. It drives steel piles deep into the ground to provide firm foundations for tall buildings. The heavy weight that drives the pile downward is raised by a motor and then released, so that it falls. When it hits the pile, it delivers a powerful inertial force, pushing the pile into the ground. Exactly the same thing happens when you hit a nail with a hammer.

Why does a sledge hammer have a long handle?

A heavy hammer, like a sledgehammer, delivers a heavy blow because its effort travels through a long distance. The bigger the head of a hammer and the longer its handle, the greater will be its impact.

Why is it harder to catch a baseball than a tennis ball thrown at the same speed?

To catch a ball, you must slow it down until it is at rest (in your hand). Your hand must get in the way and provide enough force to stop the ball's motion. A tennis ball has less mass than a baseball, so to slow it down needs a smaller force. This is the second law of motion, first put forward by Isaac Newton (although he did not play baseball, as far as we know).

How does a jet engine work?

A jet engine is an *action-reaction* engine. It shoots out a mass of hot gas, and the force of this gas pushing in one direction produces another equally strong force in the opposite direction. For every action (here, the hot gas shooting out backward), there is an equal and opposite reaction (the jet plane flying forward). Newton knew this too, even though jet planes had not been dreamed of in the 1600s. This was his third law of motion.

Exhaust nozzle

Afterburner

Compressor blades

Air inlet

Compression chamber

Turbine

Modern jet engine

What happens when two pool balls collide?

When one pool ball hits another, both balls move. They exchange *momentum*, one losing while the other gains. The momentum (the velocity, or speed, of a moving object multiplied by its mass) remains the same in total as before. As the rolling cue ball hits its target, it loses part of its velocity. Exactly the same amount of energy is transferred to the target ball.

Why does the water stay inside a bucket whirled around on the end of a rope?

If you put a little water in a plastic bucket, tie a rope firmly to the handle, and then whirl the bucket around in a circle, a surprising thing happens. The water stays inside the bucket. Why doesn't it fall out? The bucket behaves exactly as a satellite does when orbiting the Earth. It tries to escape, but is held back by the rope (just as the Earth's gravity holds back the satellite). The water inside the bucket also tries to escape outward, but is thrown against the bottom of the bucket by the force of the whirling motion.

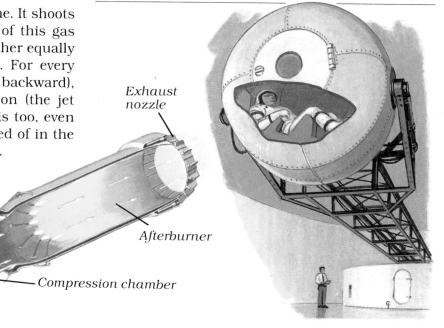

Astronauts train for lift-off in a centrifuge.

What is a centrifuge?

The inward force needed to hold a moving object in orbit is called *centripetal* force. You feel it in the rope holding the whirling bucket. When taking a corner on a bike, it seems as if you are being pulled toward the outside of the bend, so you lean over slightly the other way to counteract it. This outward-pulling force is *centrifugal* force. It is used in the centrifuge, a device used to separate cream from milk. The cream, being heavier, is thrown to the outside. The centrifuge is also used to train jet pilots and astronauts, whirling them around to experience the stresses of gravity several times greater than normal.

This skater will spin faster when she straightens and pulls her arms against her body.

Why do skaters spin faster when they draw in their arms?

A spinning object, such as a top, is spun by a combination of opposite forces known as a *couple*. If the diameter of a top is reduced, it will spin faster. When ice skaters perform a spin, they can speed up the motion by pulling their arms in against their body, so reducing their diameter.

Oil tanker and an airship

Why does wood float but lead sink?

Wood is less dense than water. When a piece of wood is dropped into water, it displaces (pushes away) only as much water as will balance its own weight. So it floats. Lead is much more dense than water. It sinks because the upthrust of the water it displaces is not enough to balance its weight.

How can an iron ship float?

A hollow object has low density because it is mostly filled with air. Even an iron ship will float in water because of the air inside. However, if a hole is put in the vessel, water pours in and pushes the air out. The overall density of the ship becomes greater than that of water and the ship sinks.

How can objects float in air?

Air is fluid, like water. But it has such a low density that few objects will float in it. Hydrogen gas is lighter than air, so a balloon filled with hydrogen is less dense than air and will rise upward. Eventually, it will reach a height where the air is so thin that the hydrogen no longer has a lower density, and it can then rise no higher.

Gravitation

Why is gravitation so important?

Force is one of three important things that scientists can measure to help us understand how the Universe works. The other two are distance and time. There are lots of forces, but the one that all bodies on Earth are affected by is gravitation, the force of gravity.

Why do things fall to earth?

Gravity is a force trying to pull us, and everything else, toward the earth. Gravity is what makes rain fall downward, and not upward. Gravity explains why if you throw a ball into the air, it will fall back to earth again. The planet Earth exerts a gravitational force on everything. But much smaller bodies also produce a similar effect. Between any two objects there is a gravitational force.

Who is supposed to have dropped weights from the top of a tower to prove that gravity affects everything equally?

The Italian scientist Galileo Galilei (1564–1642) is supposed to have climbed the Leaning Tower of Pisa to demonstrate the force of gravity. By dropping weights from the tower, he showed that all objects of similar size and shape fell at the same rate. Only air resistance affected their fall: a round weight would fall faster than a piece of cloth because its shape offered less resistance to the air. All falling objects are pulled to earth by gravity.

Galileo dropped different weights from a tower and found they landed simultaneously.

Did an apple really fall on Newton's head?

The story goes that Isaac Newton was sitting beneath an apple tree when an apple fell on his head. This set the young Newton thinking about how gravity affected everything on Earth. No one knows if the story is true, but like all great scientists Newton looked at what went on around him and then tried to work out an explanation for what he saw. So the story could well be true.

Falling skydivers reach a terminal velocity dictated by gravity and wind resistance.

How fast do falling objects fall?

The Earth's gravity makes all falling objects accelerate at 32 feet per second. In other words, for every second that an object falls, its speed increases by 32 feet per second.

How did Isaac Newton predict space travel?

In 1666 (the same year as the Great Fire of London) Isaac Newton came up with a theory of universal gravitation that explained the motion of the Moon around the Earth. He did not publish his theory until much later, in 1687. Newton reasoned that if a cannon could be fired with sufficient force, the cannonball would speed off in a straight line into space—like a spacecraft. However, no cannon could fire a cannonball fast enough to escape the Earth's gravity, so space travel had to wait until the twentieth century and the invention of the rocket engine.

Why do the planets keep moving in their orbits?

The planets have been moving ever since the formation of the solar system. They were given their starting "push" then, millions of years ago, and have kept moving ever since around the Sun. The Sun's massive gravitational force holds the planets in orbit around it. They keep moving because there is no force in the solar system powerful enough to stop them and because there is no frictional force opposing them. There is no wind resistance as in our atmosphere.

Astronauts weigh less on the Moon.

How much would you weigh on the Moon?

The weight of an object is the force of gravity acting upon it. Weight is really measured in newtons (the newton is a unit for measuring force). Mass is measured in pounds (or kilograms), and the mass of an object never changes. If you traveled to the Moon, you would weigh less than on Earth, because the Moon has only one sixth of the Earth's gravity. Even so, your mass would still be the same.

What is it like to be weightless?

No one knew what it felt like to be weightless for any length of time until the first astronauts flew in space. People inside a spacecraft orbiting the Earth float about inside, as if swimming in air. There is no Earth's gravity to pull them down. If an astronaut lets go of a tool, it will drift across the spacecraft cabin, instead of falling to the ground as it would on Earth.

Where is your center of gravity?

Everything has a center of gravity, a point of balance. In a ball, the center of gravity is in its center. Odd-shaped bodies can be made to balance unbelievably. A weighted toy, for example, will always bounce back upright because its center of gravity is so low. A thin-necked bottle will stand quite safely on its broad base. But balancing it upside down, on its neck, isn't so easy because the center of gravity is now near the top.

Their low center of gravity prevents these toys from toppling.

How can a gyroscope balance on a pencil point?

A gyroscope looks like a spinning top inside a wheel-like frame. Once set spinning, it will not alter its direction. If balanced on a pencil point, it will not fall off as long as it keeps spinning. The pull of gravity (which tries to upset the gyroscope) is countered by another force called *precession*, found in spinning bodies. This makes the gyroscope move around the point of the pencil as if it were in orbit.

Friction

What causes friction?

Friction is produced when two surfaces rub against each other. Even a smooth-looking surface is actually covered with tiny holes and bumps, as can be seen by looking at it through a microscope. The rubbing together produces heat. There is friction between the most insubstantial surfaces, such as air and water.

How can friction be reduced?

Friction is reduced if a fluid is passed between two surfaces. If you try to slide one pane of glass across another, the glass will probably stick. But if you pour water between the two panes, they will move against each other easily. The water acts as a lubricant.

How does friction help a racing car take corners at high speed?

A car, like other machines, uses bearings and lubricants (such as oil and grease) to overcome friction between its moving parts. But without friction between the car and the road, the vehicle would not move at all. A Grand Prix racing car has a low, flat body which acts like an upside-down wing. As air rushes over the car, it presses the body downward against the track. This increases friction between the track and the extra-wide tires of the car. The extra friction improves the car's road-holding, allowing the driver to take bends much faster than would be possible in an ordinary car.

What is the most common lubricant?

The lubricant used in car engines is oil. A thin layer, or film, of oil spreads over all the moving parts of the engine. Water is often used to lubricate the drilling rods used on oil rigs to find oil deposits and also to cool many types of industrial machinery. Air or gas under pressure will also act as lubricants.

How do ball bearings reduce friction?

If you have ever stepped on a marble, you will know how easily it rolls. A heavy weight can be moved quite easily if rested on some marbles. The marbles act as ball bearings. They reduce the sliding friction between the weight and the floor. Many machines have sets of ball bearings, fitted in circular "races," that allow moving parts (such as wheels) to turn freely.

An idea for a perpetual motion machine

Is a perpetual motion machine possible?

In the past many people tried to build so-called perpetual motion machines, machines that would keep working forever. Some used falling water, others magnets and rolling balls. Despite the ingenuity of such machines, none of them worked because any machine working on Earth requires some additional "input" (a force) to keep it working after it has started. Otherwise gravity and friction will eventually halt it.

Why do we need friction to walk?

Our shoes rub on the ground as we walk, producing friction. This friction gives us a "push" against the ground and so helps us to move forward. Many athletes wear shoes with ridges or spikes on the soles to give extra grip. Try walking on wet ice and you will see how hard it can be to move without friction!

Why does a spacecraft become red-hot when it reenters the Earth's atmosphere?

The atmosphere is like an invisible skin of air around the Earth. A spacecraft returning from the near-vacuum of space has to pass through this skin. As the spacecraft speeds into the atmosphere, accelerated by the pull of the Earth's gravity, it becomes hotter and hotter. This heat is caused by friction and without a heat shield to protect it, the spacecraft would be burned to cinders.

Why do car tires look flat at the bottom?

A car tire bulges outward at the point at which it rests on the road. The weight of the car presses down on the wheel, squashing the air inside the tire and pushing the tire against the road. The greater the area of tire tread touching the road, the greater the friction, and the car will be less likely to skid.

Air resistance generates massive temperatures during reentry.

Can wheels work without friction?

Engineers are constantly seeking ways to reduce friction, so as to make engines run better. But some friction is essential, or wheeled vehicles would not move at all. The wheels must get a grip on the road or rails.

Why do railway locomotives not have rubber tires like cars and trucks?

Running a vehicle on rails is actually more efficient than running it on a road. This is because a solid wheel, like that of a railway locomotive, creates less friction than an air-filled tire (as on a car), since a solid wheel does not flatten out under pressure. So it is easier to pull a heavy load along a railway track than along a road. But without some friction, to "stick" the wheels to the rails, a locomotive's wheels would spin helplessly.

French National Railway's TGV

SPACE AND TIME

When was zero first used in arithmetic?

We could not count without a figure for nothing, or zero. One way is to leave a blank, but early mathematicians soon found they needed a special symbol: 0. The zero was used by the 7th century A.D. in India and Southeast Asia and may have been used in China even earlier.

The Chinese have used the decimal system for over 3,000 years.

Who invented the decimal system?

We have ten fingers and ten toes, so counting in tens (the decimal system) seems sensible. But counting can be done in lots of other ways. As early as 1400 B.C. the Chinese used decimals. They wrote the number 365 as "three hundred plus six decades (tens) plus five days." Using decimals made it easier to work out difficult sums, but decimals did not reach Europe until the 10th century A.D.

What are negative numbers?

A negative number is one with a minus sign (−) in front of it. If 2 is two more than 0, −2 is two less than 0. Minus 20 (−20) is ten times −2, and so on. Curiously, Western mathematicians managed without minus numbers for centuries. They were unknown in Europe until the 1500s, though the Chinese used them long before.

How was the human body used in measurement?

Ancient civilizations relied on "body measurement." The smallest unit of length was the "finger" or "thumb." A cubit (the distance from a person's elbow to their fingertips) was equal to 30 fingers (roughly 18 inches in modern terms). A hand's width, normally taken as four inches, is still the unit used to measure the height of horses. According to the Bible, Goliath was six cubits and one span (about 9 inches) high so was 10 feet tall.

1 palm

1 cubit

Egyptian measurements were taken from parts of the body.

How big was an acre?

Farmers' fields are still measured in acres in many parts of the world. The metric equivalent is the hectare (equal to 2.47 acres). In the Middle Ages a furlong ("one furrow long") was the length of a field an ox could draw a plow before needing to rest. One furlong was equal to 220 yards, or 201 meters. An English acre was the area of land that could be plowed in a day: 22 furlongs.

An acre used to be how much an ox could plow in a day.

Where was the metric system first made official?

The metric (decimal) system of weights and measures was adopted in France after the French Revolution of 1789. Before then, people in Europe had used various old measures, and there was no real system. Scientists soon preferred the metric system, but Britain and the United States continued to use the Imperial system (yards, miles, pounds, gallons, and so on) in everyday life. The metric system (meters, kilometers, kilograms, liters, and so on) was introduced in Britain gradually (though by no means completely) from the 1960s.

How does geometry help us to make sense of our world?

Geometry is the branch of mathematics that has to do with the study of shapes and sizes. The name comes from Greek words meaning "Earth measurement," and it was by using geometry that Greek mathematicians first calculated the size of the Earth. Every advance in science has been aided by geometry, for without it we could not make accurate measurements. In about 300 B.C. Euclid wrote a book called *Elements* in which he brought together many of the geometrical discoveries made by Greek mathematicians. Euclid's textbook has inspired mathematicians ever since.

A magic square

8	1	6
3	5	7
4	9	2

What is meant by a geometric figure?

Every figure in geometry can be thought of as a set of points. For example, a straight line is the shortest distance between two points. A circle is a set of points, each at the same distance (the radius) from another point (the center). The study of two-dimensional (flat) figures is called plane geometry. Solid geometry deals with three-dimensional figures, such as cubes.

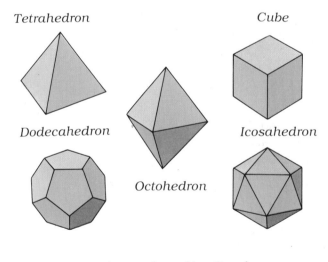

Five geometric shapes loved by Greek mathematicians.

What is a magic square?

There are lots of so-called magic squares, made of numbers that add up in an interesting way. This is a simple but very old one. It was known to the Chinese at least 3,000 years ago. The numbers in every line add up to 15—across, up and down, and diagonally.

Who invented logarithms?

Logarithms are a way of calculating, using tables. They were particularly useful before the invention of pocket calculators. Logarithms were invented in 1614 by the Scottish mathematician John Napier. He realized that numbers could be written in a kind of shorthand. For example, 16 could be written as 4^2 [4 × 4]; 64 as 4^3 [4 × 4 × 4]; and so on. By working out tables of logarithms, he was able to do long multiplication by adding the "shorthand numbers" together, and long division by subtracting them. The task of preparing his tables took Napier 20 years, beginning in 1594.

What are powers of 10?

When using very large (or very small) numbers, it is easier to use powers of 10, rather than write out lots of zeros. For example, 10 to the power 1 [10^1] is 10; 10 to the power 2 [10^2] is 100; and so on. Powers of 10 can also be used to write very small negative numbers, by adding a minus sign and an extra zero each time. So 10^{-1} is 0.1; 10^{-2} is 0.01; and so on.

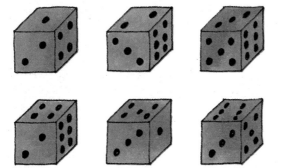

The probability of throwing any number with a die is 1:6.

How often can you expect to throw a six when playing dice?

Mathematicians have long sought ways of solving problems involving unpredictable factors, such as the fall of dice. The Frenchman Blaise Pascal worked out the basic "laws of probability" in 1642, using dice. The simplest problem is this: a die has six sides, each with a different value. When you throw it, each side has an equal chance of falling upright. The probability that one side will do so is therefore 1 in 6.

Why do numbers behave in such curious ways?

One of the fascinations of math is the odd ways in which numbers can behave. What about this puzzle, for instance? Take three 1s: 111. 1 + 1 + 1 = 3. Divide 111 by 3. The answer is 37. Now try the same calculation with 2. Three 2s: 222. 2 + 2 + 2 = 6. 222 divided by 6 equals...37! What result do you get using 3, 4, or 5?

١	٢	٣	٤	٥	٦	٧	٨	٩	٠	Arabic
1	7	3	4	4	L	7	8	9		Spanish AD 976
1	2	3	8	4	6	٨	8	9	0	W. Europe AD 1360
1	2	3	4	5	6	7	8	9	0	Italy AD 1400
1	2	3	4	5	6	7	8	9	10	0	Modern Arabic
1	2	3	4	5	6	7	8	9	10	0	Computer

Our numerals are derived from ancient Arabic.

Why were the Romans better at recording dates than doing long division?

The Romans used a different system of numerals from the ones we use today. To a Roman, counting from 1 to 10 went like this: I, II, III, IV, V, VI, VII, VIII, IX, X. L stood for 50, C for 100, D for 500, and M for 1,000. This system was all right for writing dates, but clumsy for working out sums. Because Latin continued to be used in Europe long after the end of the Roman Empire, you will often see Roman numerals used for dates on old buildings and books. In Roman numerals the year 1548, for example, was written like this:

M	D	XL	VIII
1000	500	40	8

When were Arabic numerals brought to Europe?

The Arabic numerals we use today were first used in India and reached Europe about the year A.D. 1000. A book written in 1202 by an Italian mathematician named Leonardo Fibonacci did much to persuade Europe's scientists that they must use Arabic numerals in order for the science of mathematics to progress.

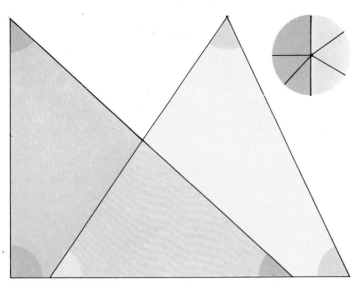

There are always 180° in a triangle, so between the blue and yellow triangles there are 360°.

Who first proved that the angles of a triangle always add up to 180 degrees?

The ancient Greeks were fascinated by geometry. They knew that a circle is made up of 360 degrees, a number probably chosen by the Babylonians. No matter what its shape, a triangle has angles that always add up to 180 degrees. This was first proved by Euclid about 300 B.C.

What was the golden mean?

The ancient Greeks were superb builders as well as mathematicians. They designed the Parthenon, one of the most famous buildings in the world, to a precise mathematical rule which they called the golden mean. The rule was that a rectangle could be any width, but its length had to be a little over one-sixth greater than the width. This would produce the most beautiful proportions, and a building with magical properties. Without calculators to aid them, the Greek architects found the exact length by making drawings. Modern mathematicians have worked out the golden mean as 1 to 1.618.

What is the biggest prime number known?

The biggest prime number found to date has 25,962 digits. There is an infinite (endless) number of prime numbers; there are more than 660,000 between 1 and 10,000,000.

Why do mathematicians hunt for prime numbers?

A prime number is one that can be divided only by itself and 1. For example, 12 is not a prime number because it can be divided by 1, 2, 3, 4 and 6. On the other hand, 11 is; it can be divided only by 1 and 11. What mystifies mathematicians about prime numbers is that they can find no pattern. A Greek named Eratosthenes worked out a slow, but effective, method of finding prime numbers. That was in the 3rd century B.C. and no one has yet found a better way.

Who could tell a prime number immediately, using a secret method?

The 17th-century French mathematician Pierre Fermat was said to have a secret "test" for finding prime numbers. He could give almost instant answers but no one knows how Fermat did this, for he died without revealing his secret.

How is the Möbius strip puzzling?

This figure is named after a 15th-century German named August Möbius, who discovered it. To make a Möbius strip, you need a strip of paper. Turn the strip a half-twist in the middle and glue the ends together to make a loop. The back surface of one end is stuck to the front surface of the other. Now try running a pencil around the strip. Has it still got a back and a front? Or does it now have only one surface? Cut the strip carefully along its middle. Have you ended up with one ring, or two?

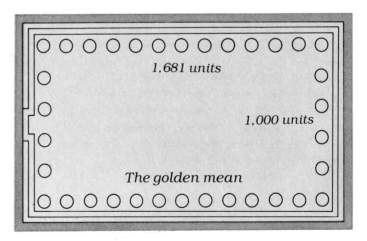

1,681 units

1,000 units

The golden mean

Measuring Time

Who counted in suns and nights?

People have measured time in a number of ways. Early people counted the days (from sunrise to sunset). But not all used the "day" as their unit. The Comanche people of the Great Plains counted in "suns"; the Greenlanders counted in "nights."

Where were flowers used as clocks?

In East Africa people grew a flower that acted as a clock. Its petals began to open as the sun rose. By noon, the petals were fully open. Then they began to close up, until by sunset they were tightly shut. Watching how far the flower was open told people the time.

How could fire be used to measure time?

Around 3000 B.C. the Chinese invented a "fire clock." It was a rod covered with tar and sawdust, cut to an exact length. At intervals along the rod were threads, each holding a ball above a gong. The rod was set on fire at sunrise and, as the flame traveled along, it burned through the threads. As each thread was burned, a ball fell and rang the gong, announcing that another hour had passed.

Fire clock

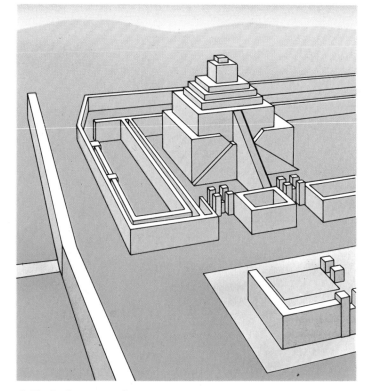

A Babylonian observatory

Who first worked out how long a year is?

More than 3,000 years ago, the priests of Babylon were skilled in astronomy and kept accurate records of the passing of the seasons. They calculated how long it took the Earth to complete one year's cycle around the Sun, and worked this out as 365 days 6 hours 15 minutes and 4 seconds. This is amazingly accurate; the modern calculation is only 26 minutes and 55 seconds longer.

Why were leap years found necessary?

The Romans based their calendar on the Moon's monthly phases. The Roman calendar started off with 360 days, but was then reduced to only 355. It became clear that the calendar was gradually getting out of step with the seasons. So Julius Caesar ordered a new calendar of 365.25 days. Every fourth year an extra day was added, to use up the quarter-days. This became a leap year. Before the new calendar could begin, an extra-long year was needed to put things straight. The year 46 B.C. had 445 days and, not surprisingly, was known as "the year of confusion."

When did people protest at having 11 days stolen from them?

The Julian calendar, named after Julius Caesar, was used until the 1500s. By then, it too was out of step. To the confusion of everyone, Easter was falling in summer instead of in spring. Pope Gregory XIII ruled that there should be a new calendar, beginning in 1582. Britain kept to the old style calendar until 1752. That year September 2 was followed by September 14 and people took to the streets, protesting that they had had 11 days stolen from their lives. Russia did not change to the Gregorian calendar until 1918; China, not until 1949.

Riots broke out when the calendar was changed in 1752.

When were sundials first used?

Sundials were used as "shadow clocks" more than 3,000 years ago in Babylonia. An upright stick casts a shadow as the Sun's rays alter position during the day. (Remember, this is because the Earth is moving, not the Sun.) Around the stick is a dial marked out with the hours.

How did water clocks work?

The ancient Egyptians and Greeks devised water clocks. The Greeks called the clock a *clepsydra*, meaning "water thief." There were various types, but they all worked on the same principle. Water dripped slowly out of a container. As the water level fell, so did a float on the surface. To the float was attached a pointer which marked the passing of the hours on a scale.

When were the first mechanical clocks invented?

Medieval monks needed to know the times for prayers during the day. They wanted a clock that would ring a bell at regular intervals. The machinery that made this possible was invented in the 1300s. Falling weights provided the force needed to ring a bell, and the fall of the weights was regulated by a mechanism known as an escapement. The escapement gave the clockwork its familiar tick-tock sound.

Were there hands on the first clocks?

Early clocks were intended only to "strike" the hours, with a bell. They were very inaccurate, losing perhaps 15 minutes a day. But people were not worried about minutes; they needed to know only what hour it was. Clocks struck every quarter hour, and that was precise enough. After all, there were no trains or buses to catch. It was not until the 1600s that clocks with minute hands and faces marked into 12 hours became common.

The Tower of the Winds in Athens was a sundial and a water clock.

How did the pendulum improve time-keeping?

A pendulum is simply a weight hung so that it can swing freely in an arc. If you set a pendulum swinging, friction will gradually shorten the distance it swings. But the time taken for each swing remains the same. In 1583 Galileo is supposed to have observed a lamp swinging in Pisa cathedral and realized this fact. The Dutch scientist Christiaan Huygens used the pendulum to regulate a clock by controlling the movement of the escapement. His pendulum clock of 1656 was much more accurate than any previous clock, to within a minute or two a day.

A pendulum such as this proved that the Earth spins.

How did a pendulum prove that the Earth was spinning?

In 1851 a French scientist named Foucault publicly demonstrated a very large pendulum in Paris. On the floor beneath the pendulum was a compass dial. The pendulum was set swinging in a north-south direction. After some time, people noticed that the motion of the swing had apparently altered, in a clockwise direction. However, as the compass dial clearly showed, it was not the pendulum that had moved, but the Earth, spinning on its own axis.

Cross staff

How did the early sailors find their way?

Few seamen in ancient times ventured out of sight of land. The Greeks invented a sundial-like device, the astrolabe, for finding longitude (east-west position), latitude (north-south), and the time of day. The astrolabe did not reach northern Europe until much later, in the 14th century.

Why did sailors need more accurate clocks to explore the vast oceans?

Finding longitude (position east-west) is more difficult than finding latitude. You need to know the exact time the Sun is overhead at different places. Galileo suggested the answer as early as 1610—a really accurate clock to keep time at sea.

How did the quest for a more reliable navigation method lead to the invention of the watch?

A pendulum clock would not keep time accurately on board a wave-tossed ship. The clock had to be freed of weights and pendulums. The answer was to use a spring, unwinding slowly, to regulate the clockwork. The British government offered a prize for the first "chronometer," or marine timekeeper. It was won in 1761 by John Harrison. His clock gained only 54 seconds during a voyage of 156 days. The spring clock had already brought another advantage: it could be made small enough to be carried in a pocket. The pocket watch had been invented.

What were the cross staff and backstaff used for?

To find their latitude (north-south position) sailors in the Middle Ages used the simple cross staff. The navigator lined up the bottom rod with the horizon and the upper rod with the Sun or a fixed star. The angle gave him the height of the Sun, and allowed him to work out roughly how far north or south of the equator the ship was. (At the equator, the Sun at noon is directly overhead, at an angle of 90°.) The backstaff, invented in 1595, was an improvement since the navigator could use it with the Sun at his back and therefore avoid being dazzled.

Time and Distance

Ptolemy's view of the Earth

Which ancient geographer believed that Earth was the center of the Universe?

Ptolemy, who lived in Egypt in the 2nd century B.C., was the leading astronomer and geographer of his time. He believed that the Earth was the center of the Universe, and that the Sun, Moon, and planets orbited around it. No one seriously challenged Ptolemy's ideas until Copernicus proved them wrong in the early 1500s.

How did Ptolemy's maps mislead later explorers?

Ptolemy tried to work out how large the Earth was, by calculating the size of each degree. However, he got it badly wrong, declaring the Earth to be 18,000 miles around, when it is actually 25,000 miles. On his map, Ptolemy made Asia seem closer to Europe than it really is. There were no better maps when, many centuries later, Christopher Columbus set sail from Spain in 1492 to find a new, western route to Asia. Columbus hoped for a short voyage and certainly did not expect to discover America.

Who divided the world into 360 degrees?

The great Greek astronomer Hipparchus (about 165–127 B.C.) was the first to divide the Earth into 360 parts, which modern geographers call degrees. The degrees measure longitude—distance east and west of the meridian (0°).

Who made the first modern-looking maps?

The same Ptolemy who got the Universe wrong actually got the Earth remarkably right! He drew a map of the world with north at the top and east on the right (just as today). He showed latitude and longitude and used different scales (so as to show more populated areas in greater detail). Following Hipparchus, he divided the globe into degrees, and further divided each degree into minutes and seconds.

Contemporary drawing showing the type of ship which took Columbus to the Americas.

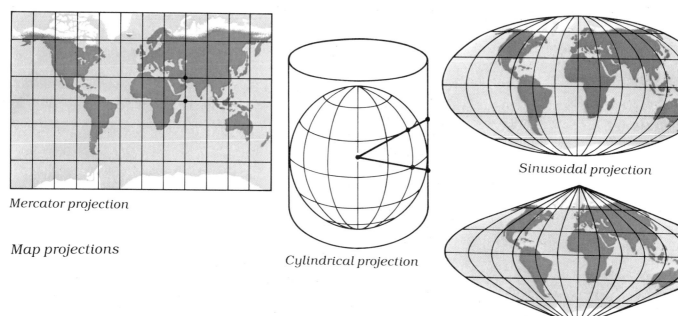

Mercator projection

Map projections

Cylindrical projection

Sinusoidal projection

Why is a flat map never really accurate?

A map in a book is flat. But the Earth is round and its features cannot be drawn accurately on a flat surface. Try peeling an orange, and you will find you cannot lay the skin out flat on a table without breaking it. Every map is drawn in a way that makes some feature (such as area) accurate, but other features (such as shape) less so. This is called a *projection*.

Why did the coming of the railroads cause timekeeping difficulties?

Railroad travel began in the 1830s. For the first time people could travel faster than a horse could run. But drawing up railroad timetables posed problems, for different parts of a country kept different time. In Britain, the famous Great Western Railway used its own "railroad time," and town clocks along its route sometimes showed both "railroad time" and local time.

When did people start using Greenwich Mean Time?

In 1880 railroad time in Britain became Greenwich time. The Royal Greenwich Observatory, near London, was by then the world's authority on timekeeping, and in 1884 it was agreed that Greenwich Mean Time should set the standard for time all over the world.

What is the Greenwich meridian?

If you visit Greenwich, England, you can stand with one foot in the Eastern Hemisphere and the other in the Western Hemisphere. The Greenwich (or prime) meridian (0° longitude) was adopted in 1884. France wanted the 0° line to pass through Paris, but Greenwich won the day because since 1850 it had had a special telescope used for navigational observations. The British Astronomer Royal, Sir George Biddell Airy, suggested that this telescope should serve as the meridian. Since 1884 all maps have shown the line of 0° longitude running through Greenwich.

Why do air travelers have to change their watches?

The world is divided into 24 time zones. The time in each zone differs by one hour from the time in the next. East of Greenwich in England (where it is Greenwich Mean Time, or GMT), the time is later. West of Greenwich, the time is earlier; noon in Greenwich is 7 A.M. (five hours earlier) in New York and 3 P.M. (three hours later) in Moscow. The United States covers five time zones: Atlantic, Eastern, Central, Mountain, and Pacific. Airline passengers flying west have to put their watches back on landing. Flying east, they must put their watches forward.

Measuring the Past

When was B.C. and A.D. dating introduced?

There are many different systems for dating. Muslims begin their calendar from the Hegira, the flight of Muhammad from Mecca in A.D. 622. The Christian calendar, now widely used worldwide, begins with the birth of Jesus. Dates before then are followed by the letters B.C. (for "before Christ"). Dates after then are prefixed by the letters A.D. (Latin *Anno Domini*, or "in the year of the Lord"). A.D. dating was suggested by a monk-mathematician named Dionysius Exiguus in the year 525. It was much later that B.C. was used, in the 1600s.

Who believed the Earth was less than 5,000 years old?

In the 1600s many people believed that the Earth's age could be worked out from the facts and family trees given in the Bible. Using this method, Archbishop James Ussher (1581–1656) calculated that the date of the Creation had been 4004 B.C. Not even such a great scientist as Sir Isaac Newton imagined that the Earth was in fact millions and millions of years older.

Who first suggested that there had been a Stone Age, a Bronze Age, and an Iron Age?

Interest in "prehistory" really began in the 1700s and 1800s. People began exploring ruins and digging up old weapons, cooking pots, and coins. It was the beginning of the modern science of archaeology. A Danish museum curator named Christian Thomsen was given the task of sorting out piles of such finds, called antiquities. He sorted them into groups of stone objects, bronze objects, and iron objects. It occurred to him that the stone objects might be older than the others. In 1836 Thomsen wrote a book about his work, in which he suggested that there had been "Three Ages" of prehistory—the Stone Age, the Bronze Age, and the Iron Age.

How do modern archaeologists measure time?

Today archaeologists uncover the past layer by layer. Objects can be dated by the radiocarbon method (measuring the amount of radioactive carbon 14 left in charcoal, wood, or animal bones). The study of tree growth-rings also helps them, especially using the wood of the bristlecone pine of California. This is the oldest living thing on Earth, reaching ages of up to 4,600 years. Tree-ring dating has helped to correct errors in radiocarbon dates.

What have been the greatest treasures uncovered by archaeologists?

There have been many valuable finds since Heinrich Schliemann excited the world in the 1870s by discovering the remains of the ancient city of Troy. In 1899 Arthur Evans discovered the Minoan civilization of Knossos on the island of Crete. In 1922 Lord Carnarvon and Howard Carter entered the undisturbed tomb of the Egyptian boy-king Tutankhamen. In 1979 Chinese archaeologists uncovered the tomb of the emperor Qin Shi Huang Di (reigned 221–210 B.C.). Inside was a buried army of 6,000 life-sized terra cotta warriors, each different from the rest.

Emperor Qin's terra cotta warriors

Space and Time

How did the search for a mysterious substance called ether reveal something new about light?

In the 1800s scientists wondered if light rays were carried through space by a mysterious "ether"— just as sound travels through air. Two American scientists, Albert Michelson and Edward Morley, did an experiment in 1881 to detect ether using a telescope and mirrors. They wanted to see if light rays were slowed down by the ether as the Earth moved through space. Their experiment found that there was no ether. It revealed an unexpected fact: the speed of light is always the same.

Who changed the way people understand time?

Albert Einstein (1879–1955) was the greatest scientific thinker of modern times. Einstein reasoned that for an object traveling very fast, time is different from that experienced by someone standing still. Before, people had followed Isaac Newton (who thought time could never change) or other thinkers such as Immanuel Kant in the late 1700s (who believed time did not really exist, except in our minds). Einstein explained the results of the Michelson-Morley experiment (*see previous question*): it was not the speed of light that varied, but time itself.

What is "relative motion"?

Imagine two spacecraft approaching one another. Each is traveling at 12,500 miles per hour (mph). Their closing speed, *relative* to one another, is twice as great: 25,000 mph. If one scientist on Earth and another scientist on one of the speeding spacecraft were to measure the speed of the light reaching them from the Sun, they would obtain the same figure: around 186,000 miles per second. This example illustrates two points central to Einstein's theories about relativity: first, all motion is relative; and second, the velocity of light is always the same.

Can anything travel faster than light?

Einstein published his special theory of relativity in 1905. He believed that length, mass, and time were all affected by motion; and he thought that nothing could travel faster than the speed of light. Near the speed of light, mass would be infinite, length would be zero, and time would slow down almost to a stop.

Why might future space travelers return to find their children older than they were?

The faster an object travels, the slower time passes for it. If future astronauts could travel to distant stars at speeds much higher than are yet possible, very odd things would happen. If they were away ten years, they might return to find that 40 years had passed on Earth. An astronaut who was 25 when she left, saying good-bye to her daughter of three, would return aged 35 to find her daughter was 43!

What are the most accurate clocks ever made?

Atomic clocks keep the most accurate time. These are based on the vibration rate of certain atoms or molecules. Most atomic clocks use the vibrations of a cesium atom to regulate quartz crystals. Some scientific clocks are accurate to one second in a million years.

All motion is relative.

Astronomy

How did a solar eclipse prove another of Einstein's theories?

In 1916, in his general theory of relativity, Einstein examined the effects of acceleration and gravity. He believed that light was bent not only by traveling through different mediums but also by gravity. In 1919 there was an eclipse of the Sun. Observers saw that stars near the edge of the Sun seemed to alter position. The light from the stars was being bent by the Sun's gravity. Einstein was right.

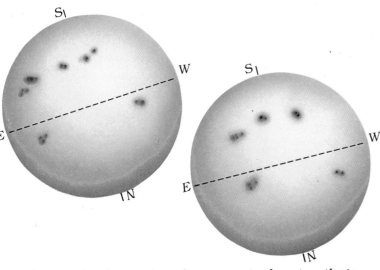

Sunspots, drawn two days apart, showing their movement.

Why did medieval astronomers refuse to believe their eyes when they saw sunspots?

Sunspots, looking like darker patches, appear and disappear on the surface of the Sun. They can be seen with the naked eye, and Chinese astronomers studied them as early as 300 B.C. European astronomers did not know what to make of sunspots. Since they believed the Sun was a "perfect sphere" in the heavens, they could not accept that there were any "imperfections" on its surface. [NEVER LOOK AT THE SUN DIRECTLY WITH THE NAKED EYE OR THROUGH A LENS. The Sun's light is powerful enough to damage your eyes.]

Why did the ideas of Copernicus create a furious argument?

The Polish astronomer Nicolaus Copernicus (or Mikolaj Kopernik) published a book in 1543 that upset many people's ideas about the Universe. Copernicus declared that Ptolemy's theory, that the Earth was the center of the Universe, could not be right. Other Greek scientists had suggested that the Earth traveled around the Sun, and Copernicus agreed with them. In his book Copernicus showed a drawing of the solar system, with the Sun at its center and the five known planets circling it. Beyond, in an outer ring, were the stars. Many people were alarmed by these new ideas because they seemed to make the Earth, and humankind, less important in the Universe.

Who caused a sensation when he found a new star?

In 1572 the Danish astronomer Tycho Brahe spotted a star he had never seen before. He observed it for 18 months and clearly saw it twinkle and change color. Believing it to be a new star, Tycho called it a "nova." But the common belief among scientists of the day was that the stars were fixed in their places and had been so since the world had been created. The discovery of Tycho's nova made people realize that in fact the Universe was constantly changing.

Tycho Brahe

What is a supernova?

Tycho's nova was in fact not a new star, but an old star suddenly flaring up and becoming much brighter. Such stars are now known as supernovas, and in our own Milky Way galaxy, only four have been recorded, most recently in 1987 in the southern sky. The other three were spotted in 1054, 1572, and 1604.

Who first used a telescope to study the heavens?

The Italian scientist Galileo learned of the invention of the telescope and built one for himself about 1610. With his telescope, Galileo discovered a Universe far larger than anyone had imagined. He could see "ten times as many stars." He discovered four moons of Jupiter. Turning his telescope on our own Moon, he saw that it had a rough surface, pitted with craters.

Who believed the Moon must be inhabited?

Johannes Kepler (1571–1630) was the first scientist to prove that the planets moved around the Sun not in circles but in oval, or elliptical, orbits. When he heard of Galileo's discoveries, he declared that the craters on the Moon must be circular walled cities built by Moon people. Kepler thought the Moon people were probably giants, 19 times larger than humans!

Who took the first photographs of the Moon?

John Draper of the United States took the first astronomical photographs of the Moon in 1840. This was not long after the invention of photography. Today astronomers observe distant stars using computers and television cameras. A photographic plate exposed for several hours can collect the very faint light from a distant star, too far away to be seen through the largest optical telescope.

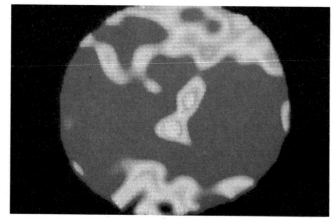

Computer-enhanced image of the Sun

What are light-years and parsecs?

Space is so vast that ordinary units of measurement such as the mile are of little use. Scientists measure the Universe in light-years and parsecs. A light-year is the distance light travels in a year: about 6 trillion miles. A parsec is roughly 3.25 light-years (one parsec equals 19.6 trillion miles).

Which star is closest to the Earth?

The star Proxima Centauri is the closest to us, at a distance of 4.2 light-years. Next closest are Alpha Centauri (4.3 light-years) and Barnard's star (6 light-years).

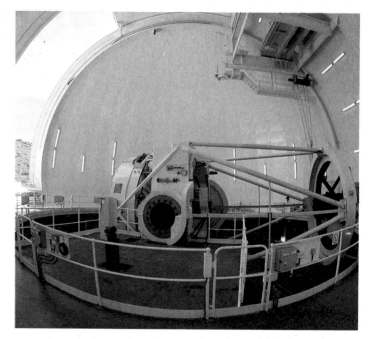

Inside a large telescope

How are astronomers gazing into the past when they study the stars?

Light reaching us from even the closest stars has taken several years to cross the enormous distances of space. The nearest star is more than four light-years away, so the light from it takes four years to reach us. This means we see the star as it looked four years ago. Other stars are millions of light-years away. So when astronomers study light from these stars, they are seeing them as they were millions of years ago.

What are asteroids?

Asteroids are minor planets orbiting the Sun between the orbits of Mars and Jupiter. The largest is called Ceres and was discovered in 1801. It is about 600 miles across. Most asteroids are much smaller.

Could we send spacecraft to the stars?

The stars are so far away that travel to them is out of the question—at least for the foreseeable future. The fastest spacecraft yet built would take more than 150,000 years to reach the closest star.

Will the Sun grow hotter or colder as it ages?

The surface temperature of the Sun is about 10,112°F. The Sun is an "average" star, in terms of its size and brightness. Thousands of millions of years from now, it will swell up to become a "red giant," perhaps 100 times its present size. Life on Earth will become impossible, and the planet itself may even be engulfed by the gigantic Sun. In time, the red giant Sun will shrink and become a tiny, very dense star called a "white dwarf." As its life ends, it will gradually cool and become invisible.

How old is the Universe?

The Universe is at least 15,000 million years old, and probably older. Scientists work out the age by measuring the rate at which distant stars have cooled down since the Universe began. Recently, some scientists have suggested that stars may cool down more slowly than was thought, so the Universe may be much older than was once believed.

How did the Universe begin?

Many scientists think that the Universe came into being with a huge explosion known as the "big bang." The explosion sent matter flying apart, and the Universe has continued to expand ever since. Radio astronomers have picked up radiation that does not seem to come from any single source, but is spread throughout space. They believe this radiation may be the result of the big bang.

What is the most distant object in space that we can see without using a telescope?

The great spiral galaxy of Andromeda can be seen as a faint cloud in space. It is a spiral galaxy, like our own Milky Way, made up of millions of stars. Andromeda is 2.2 million light-years away, the farthest object visible from Earth with the naked eye.

Where are we in our own galaxy?

The Milky Way is made up of many millions of stars, of which our own Sun is just one. The galaxy stretches across the night sky like a milky cloud. In the past, people thought of it as the pathway to heaven. If you imagine the galaxy as a wheel lying on its side, with the hub as its center, the Sun lies roughly two-thirds of the way out toward the rim. The whole galaxy measures 100,000 light-years across and is spinning in space.

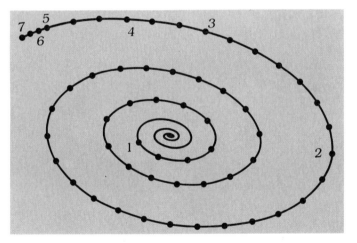

The age of the Universe: 1. 10–35 seconds after the big bang; 2. 100 seconds on, helium forms; 3. 10,000 years, matter begins; 4. 100,000 years, stars form; 5. A billion years, Earth born; 6. 10 billion years, life on Earth; 7. Humans appear.

How many stars are there?

There are just too many stars for us to count. There are billions and billions of stars in the Universe, and scientists have not yet discovered any limit to the size of the Universe. Our own Milky Way galaxy is a fairly ordinary star system. Yet it contains 100,000 million stars. There are much, much larger galaxies.

THE EARTH

Where did the Earth come from?

Once it was thought that the Earth and planets were formed from the Sun. Now most scientists agree that the Sun and planets, including the Earth, were formed at the same time. A whirling cloud of dust and gas gathered in space and grew denser under the force of its own gravity. Most of the huge cloud formed the Sun. The remains formed the planets.

What is the Earth made of?

The outer surface of the Earth is a thin crust of rock about 30 miles deep at its thickest. The crust is only 4 miles thick in some places under the ocean. Beneath the crust is hot, partly melted rock. This is the *mantle*, nearly 1,800 miles thick. Next comes an outer core of melted metals and then a solid inner core of metal, possibly iron and nickel.

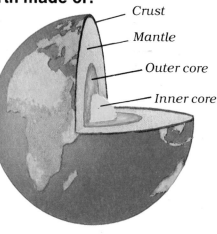

Crust

Mantle

Outer core

Inner core

Where is the lithosphere?

The lithosphere is another name for the Earth's crust. It is sometimes used to include the mantle and core as well.

How old is the Earth?

The Earth is about 4,600 million years old. Scientists have worked this out by studying rocks in meteorites which have landed on Earth from outer space. Meteorites are lumps of rock which were formed at the same time as the Earth. Scientists have also calculated the Earth's age from the rate at which the radioactive metal uranium decays into lead (*see page 9*).

Is the Earth perfectly round?

The ancient Greeks and Chinese believed the Earth to be round. Observers seeing a ship's mast appearing over the horizon before the rest of the vessel must have guessed at the Earth's round shape in order to explain what they saw. In fact, the Earth is not perfectly round, but is flattened slightly at the poles because of the speed at which it spins.

What keeps the Earth in place?

Like other planets, the Earth is held in a path, or orbit, around the Sun. The Sun's gravity is the force which holds the Earth in place.

Has a day on Earth always lasted 24 hours?

The Earth spins on its own axis once in just under 24 hours. As it spins, the side which faces the Sun has day, and the other half of the Earth has night. The speed at which the Earth is spinning has gradually slowed down. A day on Earth 400 million years ago lasted only 22 hours, as it then took only 22 hours for the Earth to turn once on its axis.

Why do we have summer and winter?

The four seasons—spring, summer, autumn, and winter—are caused because the Earth is tilted on its axis (the imaginary line which passes through the North and South poles). As the Earth orbits the Sun, the part of the Earth tilted toward the Sun is warm and has summer; the part tilted away from the Sun has winter. By the end of a year, or 365 days, the Earth has completed one orbit of the Sun.

Are the Earth's magnetic poles always in the same position?

Today, the north magnetic pole of the Earth lies in northern Canada. It has been in different places in the past. The south magnetic pole, now in Antarctica, was in the Sahara 450 million years ago. The magnetic poles never stray far from the geographical North and South poles.

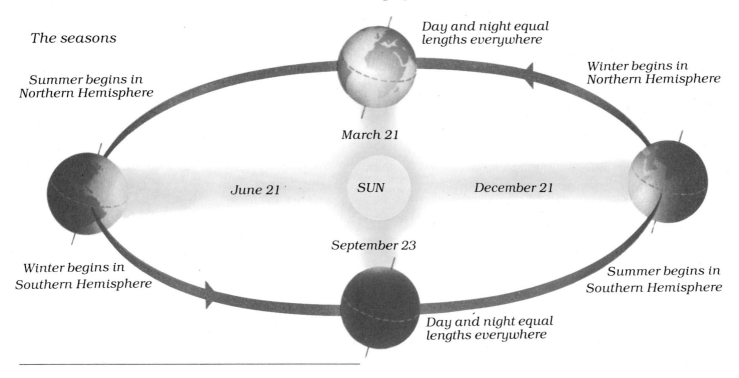

The seasons

Summer begins in Northern Hemisphere

Day and night equal lengths everywhere

Winter begins in Northern Hemisphere

March 21

June 21   *SUN*   *December 21*

September 23

Winter begins in Southern Hemisphere

Summer begins in Southern Hemisphere

Day and night equal lengths everywhere

Are the North and South poles the same as the Earth's magnetic poles?

The Earth is a huge magnet which has north and south poles. They are close to the geographic North and South poles, but not the same.

Who was the first person to measure the Earth?

The ancient Greek scientist Eratosthenes measured the Earth's circumference in the third century B.C. He did it by measuring the angle of the Sun's rays at different places some distance apart. Using geometry, he then worked out the Earth's circumference almost exactly. He said it was 252,000 stadia (28,969 miles). The modern figure is 24,902 miles at the equator.

The magnetic poles are neither fixed nor at the geographic poles.

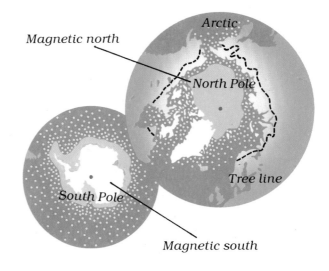

Magnetic north

Arctic

North Pole

Tree line

South Pole

Magnetic south

Have there always been seven continents on the Earth?

All seven continents on the Earth today—Africa, Asia, Antarctica, Australasia, Europe, North and South America—were once part of one gigantic supercontinent called Pangaea. Pangaea existed more than 200 million years ago. It had itself been formed by smaller landmasses colliding. About 100 million years ago, Pangaea started to break up, to form the continents we know today. By looking at a map of the world, you can tell where the continents may once have been joined.

The world today

100 million years ago

200 million years ago

What is the biosphere?

The biosphere is the Earth's "skin" of soil, water, and air. Within it live all the planet's plants and animals. No other planet in the solar system has such a biosphere.

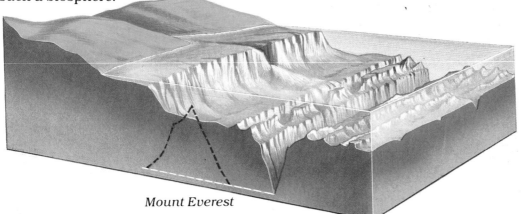

Mount Everest

The ocean floor

How can continents move?

The Earth's crust is formed of a number of separate curved plates. The plates float like giant rafts on a thick mass of molten rock. Heat from within the Earth sends currents moving through this molten rock, and these currents cause the plates to move. As the plates move, so do the continents resting on them.

Is Mount Everest getting higher?

In some places, patches of continental crust collide as one plate pushes up another. The Indian subcontinent was once separate from the rest of Asia. It was pushed northward and collided with Asia. The force of the collision pushed rocks upward to make mountains. This is how the Himalayas were formed. Because this movement is continuing, the Himalayas are still being pushed very slowly upward, and Mount Everest is getting higher.

Which is oldest: land or sea?

The rocks of the continents are up to 3,800 million years old. The oldest rocks in the ocean crust are much younger, less than 200 million years old. The youngest rocks are found near undersea ridges, where new crust is constantly being pushed up from beneath the Earth.

Where is the deepest point of the ocean?

The Earth's oceanic crust moves all the time. In the Pacific, the crust disappears into deep trenches at the edge of the ocean. There are no similar trenches in the Atlantic Ocean. The deepest trench on Earth is the Mariana in the western Pacific, which is 6.8 miles deep: more than deep enough to swallow Mount Everest.

What causes earthquakes and volcanoes?

Nearly all big earthquakes happen at the edges of the plates which make up the Earth's crust, as one plate moves underneath or slips past another. Active volcanoes are found in areas where new oceanic crust is squeezed up from deep inside the Earth, as in Iceland, or in areas where the crust is disappearing down beneath the continents, as in the Andes mountains of South America.

What makes a volcano erupt?

A volcano is a vent, or hole, in the Earth's crust. Through the vent, hot molten rocks from deep in the Earth pour out onto the surface. A volcano acts as a "safety valve," releasing pressure that has built up below in the Earth. There are about 850 active volcanoes (ones that may erupt, and may also give off steam or make rumbling noises). Other volcanoes are classed as dormant or extinct.

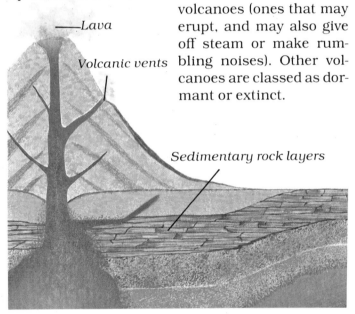

Section through a volcano

What is measured by the Richter scale?

The Richter scale is used by scientists to compare the strength of earthquakes. An earthquake is a sudden movement, or break, in the Earth's crust caused by a build-up of stresses in rocks. They cause a series of shocks, or tremors. The Richter scale ranges from 0 to 10. At 2, a person would feel a tremor in the ground. At 6, buildings would be damaged. The largest shock ever recorded measured 8.9 on the Richter scale.

What are magma and lava?

Inside the Earth, molten rock is called *magma*. When it flows onto the surface as a result of a volcanic eruption, it is called *lava*. Molten lava is almost white-hot, reaching a temperature of 2,192°F. On the surface, it cools and hardens.

Why do geysers spout hot water and steam?

Geysers are found in areas of volcanic activity, such as Iceland. Hot volcanic rocks near the surface of the Earth heat water, producing hot springs. If more water deeper down gets hot enough to turn to steam, it pushes up the water above it to form a spout or geyser. Geysers can blow out with tremendous force. Old Faithful, a famous geyser in Yellowstone National Park, Wyoming, erupts for about five minutes every hour.

Geyser

How could a fisherman not notice a wave powerful enough to smash buildings on shore?

Tsunamis (the name is Japanese) are giant ocean waves created by movement of the seafloor, such as a severe earthquake. Tsunamis happen mostly in the Pacific Ocean. The wave crests may be hundreds of miles apart and travel very fast (up to 500 mph). But in the open ocean the waves are not high enough to disturb a small boat. Only when tsunamis enter shallow water do their waves grow to enormous height. It is a curious fact that tsunamis, which caused great damage and loss of life on shore, have passed unnoticed beneath the boats of fishermen in deep water.

Rocks

What are the Earth's rocks made of?

The Earth's crust is made up of rock. Rocks are solid clusters of minerals (chemical substances composed of crystals). The minerals quartz, feldspar, and mica are found in granite, for example.

How does mud become rock?

Sedimentary rocks start off as sediment (mud and sand) washed down by rivers to the beds of lakes and seas. Shells, animal remains, and minerals may all form part of this sediment. The mixture then gradually hardens into rock as it is buried beneath more and more layers of sediment. Most sedimentary rocks are therefore made from fragments of older rocks which form the mud and sand of their sediments. Chalk, a form of limestone, is a sedimentary rock made millions of years ago mostly from the skeletons of sea creatures.

The Giant's Causeway in Ireland is made of thousands of six-sided rocks.

What are metamorphic rocks?

Metamorphosis means "change," and metamorphic rocks are formed when existing rocks are affected by heat, pressure, or chemical changes. Some rocks may be heated by molten magma passing through them. Rocks under mountains may be pressed by the forces pushing up the mountains. An example of a metamorphic rock is marble, which is made from limestone squeezed and heated deep inside the Earth.

Chalk cliffs

Why do rocks have faults?

Rocks are squeezed and folded by the enormously strong movements of the Earth's crust. Cracks, or fractures, appear in rocks as they are squeezed or as they cool down. If rock on either side of a fracture moves, the fracture becomes a fault. Earthquakes may happen when rocks on either side of a fault move quickly. During the 1906 San Francisco earthquake, the San Andreas fault moved more than 20 feet at one point.

How long ago was coal formed?

Coal is the remains of long-dead vegetation. The oldest coal we mine today was formed in swampy forests 345 million to 225 million years ago. The decaying vegetation was buried and squashed to form layers, or seams, of coal.

Water and Ice

How much of the Earth's surface is covered by ocean?

The total area of the Earth's surface is 196,949,970 square miles. The amount covered by ocean is just under 71 percent.

How much of the Earth's water is frozen into ice?

About 2.5 percent of the water on the Earth is permanently frozen. Ice sheets cover about 10.5 percent of the world's land surface.

How thick is the ice at the South Pole?

Nine tenths of all the world's ice is in the southern continent of Antarctica. Around the South Pole is a massive ice sheet, with an average thickness of 6,600 feet. At its thickest, the polar ice is more than 15,700 feet deep (enough to cover the peak of Mont Blanc, Europe's highest mountain).

What is a glacier?

A glacier is a moving "river" of ice. Glaciers are found in polar regions and in high mountains, wherever more snow falls in winter than is lost through melting and evaporation in summer. The icy mass creeps slowly downhill. When a glacier reaches the sea in very cold regions, huge blocks of ice break off to form floating icebergs.

Atlantic

Pacific

The Pacific Ocean covers almost half the globe.

Where does a glacier end in a semi-tropical forest?

The Franz Josef glacier is in the Southern Alps of New Zealand. It descends from Mount Cook into a warm, green fern forest where it melts. There are other glaciers in tropical Africa and South America, in mountains so high that snow lies all year round.

How fast can a glacier move?

The surface of a glacier moves faster than its base. Normally a glacier moves no quicker than 6 feet a day. The Quaraya glacier in Greenland, which covers 78 feet a day, is usually reckoned to be the world's fastest. But there are other "surging" glaciers that suddenly speed up and advance at up to 390 feet a day. These surges last for a year or so, and then the glacier may remain still for up to 100 years.

Glacier

Has the Earth ever been completely free of ice?

During its history, the Earth has had warm and cold spells. During the cold spells, known as ice ages, much of the Earth's surface has been covered by snow and ice. At other times, the planet has been much warmer. Trees once grew in Antarctica, for example. But from studying evidence of prehistoric ice in ancient rocks, scientists think that there has probably always been some ice at the North and South poles.

Mammoths

Could the Antarctic once have been tropical?

Scientists have found that the rocks of Antarctica contain coal (formed from long-dead plants) and other fossilized remains. These show that the climate in Antarctica was once much warmer and wetter than today. Its rocks are similar to rocks found in Australia, South America, Africa, and India. This suggests that all these continents were once joined.

When was the last Ice Age?

The most recent Ice Age began about 1.6 million years ago. Ice sheets piled up in Scandinavia and spread south to cover the British Isles, much of northern Germany and the USSR, all of Canada, and the northern part of the US. About 10,000 years ago the ice retreated. Since the last Ice Age began, there have been 17 extra-cold spells, called glacials, separated by warmer interglacial periods. Many scientists believe we are living in one of these warmer interglacials. There have been other ice ages during the millions of years of the Earth's existence.

Why are there fjords in Scandinavia?

Glaciers and ice sheets grind and cut into the landscape across which they move. Glaciers seek out the easiest path down a mountain, such as a river valley. The ice widens and deepens the valley, and after the ice melts, water flows into it from the sea. This is how the deep, narrow inlets called fjords were formed. There are many fjords in Scandinavia and others in Chile and Alaska.

A fjord in Norway carved out by an ancient glacier.

What is permafrost?

In Antarctica, Alaska, parts of Canada, and the USSR, the ground is frozen all year round. In Siberia, this frozen layer, called permafrost, is almost 2,000 feet thick. The surface thaws in summer, but the layers beneath stay frozen. The surface refreezes in autumn. Preserved bodies of extinct mammoths have been discovered in permafrost.

Oceans

What causes ocean currents?

The main movements in the world's oceans are currents caused by wind. As they blow in their regular patterns over the oceans, winds blow water particles along. The movement spreads through the water, forming currents. Currents move faster in the west of oceans than in the east. This is a result of the world's wind directions and the spin of the Earth.

How does the Gulf Stream keep Britain warm in winter?

The Gulf Stream is a warm water current which begins in the Gulf of Mexico, on the east coast of North America. The warm current flows eastward across the Atlantic Ocean and affects the climate of western Europe. This is why Labrador in eastern Canada has much colder winters than Britain, although both are equally north of the equator.

The cause of large waves is unusually high winds.

What makes waves in the sea?

The wind causes most waves. Wave size depends on three things: the area of the water surface over which the wind blows, the speed of the wind, and the length of time the wind blows. A hurricane does not necessarily produce the largest sea waves because winds in a hurricane keep changing direction. A wave breaks when the water at its crest starts moving faster than the rest of the wave, toppling over on itself.

Why is seawater salty?

The sea contains minerals washed into it from the land by rivers. The rivers dissolve minerals from the rocks over which they flow. The most plentiful mineral in the sea is salt, or sodium chloride. As the Sun's heat evaporates seawater, what remains becomes even saltier. This is why the Dead Sea (which evaporates rapidly because it is surrounded by hot desert) is so salty.

What is the continental shelf?

At the edge of most continents, the sea is shallow. Below the water lies a broad strip of seabed known as the continental shelf. The shelf is up to 660 feet deep and is made from the same rocks as the land. Beyond it lies the steeper continental slope, which drops down to the abyssal plain, or seafloor, 2.5 miles below the surface.

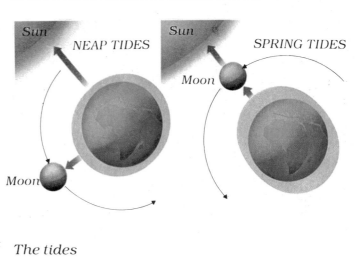

The tides

What makes the tide go in and out?

Ocean tides come in (flood) and go out (ebb) about twice every 24 hours. Tides are caused by the gravitational pull of the Sun and Moon on the Earth. The Moon is nearer to Earth than the Sun so has the stronger pull. When Moon and Sun are pulling together on the same side of the Earth, ocean tides are highest. These are called spring tides. When Sun and Moon pull against one another, neap tides (the lowest) occur. We notice this gravitational effect of the Earth's oceans because water moves easily, but the planet's land masses are also pulled in the same way.

Atmosphere and Weather

Where does the Earth's atmosphere begin and end?

The Earth is surrounded by a thin layer of gases called the atmosphere, which can be imagined as the peel covering an apple. It is this shallow layer that makes life possible on our planet. Gravity presses most of the gases of the atmosphere (including the oxygen we breathe) close to the Earth's surface. But the air grows thinner the farther it is from the ground. At 5.5 miles (the height of Mount Everest) the air is only one third as dense as at sea level. Above 500 miles it thins even more rapidly, until only a few molecules of helium and hydrogen remain. The atmosphere gradually merges with space.

What are the Van Allen belts?

Far out on the fringes of the atmosphere are two doughnut-shaped zones of radiation known as the Van Allen belts. They are made of electrically charged particles held in place by the Earth's magnetic field. The belts are strongest over the equator and weakest over the poles. The belts were discovered by the US *Explorer 1* satellite in 1958 and named after James Van Allen, who designed the experiment that found them. The belts shield the Earth from harmful cosmic rays coming from space.

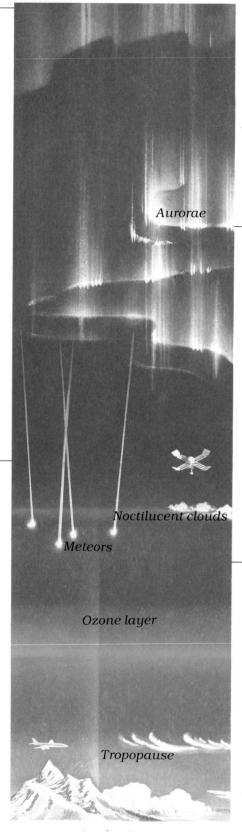

Aurorae

Noctilucent clouds

Meteors

Ozone layer

Tropopause

What does the atmosphere do?

The troposphere contains most of the world's weather and the air that we breathe. The stratosphere contains most of the atmosphere's ozone, which absorbs harmful ultraviolet radiation from the Sun. Without the ionosphere, we could not have worldwide radio broadcasting. This layer reflects radio waves, "bouncing" them around the curved surface of the Earth.

Why is there a hole above Antarctica?

Around the Earth is a layer of the gas ozone (a form of oxygen). This layer shields us from harmful ultraviolet rays given off by the Sun. Scientists have discovered that there is a hole in the ozone layer above Antarctica; it appears during the winter and closes up again in summer. They believe the hole may indicate that air pollution, and especially the release of certain chemicals from aerosol sprays, is damaging the ozone layer.

How many layers does the atmosphere have?

The atmosphere has five main layers. These are the *troposphere* (up to 10.5 miles); the *stratosphere* (up to 31 miles); the *mesosphere* (up to 53 miles); the *thermosphere* (up to 310 miles); and lastly the *exosphere* (above 310 miles). The thermosphere is also known as the *ionosphere*. This is the start of outer space.

By what names are the polar lights better known?

The polar lights are known as the aurora borealis (in the Northern Hemisphere) and the aurora australis (in the Southern Hemisphere). They are caused by flares or explosions on the Sun, which send out millions of energized particles (electrons and protons). Approaching the Earth, most of these particles are absorbed by the Van Allen belts. But at the poles (where the belts are weakest) they hit the atmosphere and their impact sometimes produces a brilliant display of colored lights in the sky.

Why do some countries have monsoons?

A monsoon is a seasonal wind. It blows from sea to land in summer, and from land to sea in winter. In lands near the equator, the air grows very hot in summer. It expands and thins out. Cooler and denser air from over the sea is sucked inland, carrying moisture on the wind. This moisture falls as torrential rain, vital to the growth of each year's crops. In India the monsoon lasts from three to four months.

Why does it rain?

Water is constantly being exchanged between the land and the atmosphere. We call this the "water cycle." Water from lakes, rivers, seas, and plants is evaporated by the Sun's heat to form water vapor. This vapor is held in the air. Air rises when warm, when forced upward by mountains, or when it meets a heavier mass of cold air. The rising air cools, and some water vapor condenses back into water droplets which mass together to form clouds. As the air rises higher, more vapor turns to water and the clouds grow bigger and darker. When the droplets grow too large to be held in the clouds they fall as rain.

What is St. Elmo's fire?

An odd form of natural electricity is sometimes seen by sailors and pilots. A glowing light plays around the masts of a ship or the antennas and wing tips of aircraft. It is also sometimes seen around lightning rods. The light is known as St. Elmo's fire (after St. Elmo or Erasmus, patron saint of Mediterranean sailors).

Can there really be a blue moon?

Very high clouds of dust and smoke in the atmosphere (from a violent volcanic eruption or huge forest fires, for instance) can affect the light rays which pass through it from the Sun. This happens very rarely. When it does, the Sun and Moon can appear to be green or even blue.

Why are lands near the equator so hot?

The equator is an imaginary line around the middle of the Earth. Near the equator, the Sun's rays shine straight down onto the Earth. Farther from the equator, the Sun's rays hit the Earth at an angle and must pass through a thicker layer of atmosphere (up to four times greater at the poles than at the equator). The thicker atmosphere absorbs more of the Sun's heat. So the hottest places on Earth are near the equator.

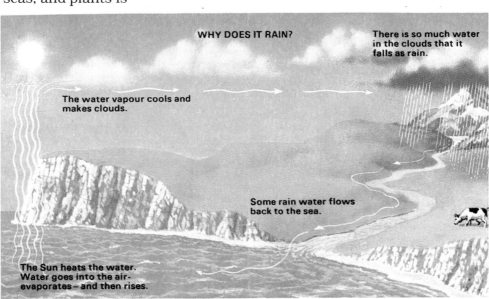

WHY DOES IT RAIN?

There is so much water in the clouds that it falls as rain.

The water vapour cools and makes clouds.

Some rain water flows back to the sea.

The Sun heats the water. Water goes into the air – evaporates – and then rises.

What makes winds blow?

Winds are movements of air across the Earth's surface. They are mostly caused by differences in temperature. The air at the equator gets the most warmth from the Sun; it expands and rises. Cooler air from the North and South poles moves in to take its place. The result is a pattern of winds. Changing temperatures over land and sea also affect the pattern of winds. Regular winds blowing toward the equator are known as trade winds.

Where might you have stepped into a puddle almost 6.5 feet deep after a day's rainfall?

On the Indian Ocean island of Réunion in 1952 an amazing 73.6 inches of rain fell in 24 hours. That is enough to cover a tall adult and the most rainfall ever recorded in a single day.

Hurricanes can uproot trees and cause extensive damage to buildings.

Where do hurricanes happen?

The violent storms known as hurricanes occur in the tropics (regions of the Earth on or near the equator). The storms form over the ocean as moist air is sucked up into a spiraling storm cloud. At the center, or "eye," of the hurricane, it is quite calm. But on the outside there are thunderstorms, lashing winds, and rain. Hurricanes cause great damage when they are blown inshore, but soon die down over land because there is not enough moisture to feed them.

How does a barometer forecast the weather?

A barometer measures air pressure. The commonest kind is called an aneroid barometer. It has a drum from which almost all the air has been removed (creating a near-vacuum). Changes in air pressure make the drum expand or contract, which causes a pointer to move around a dial. Clear and settled weather is likely when the pressure is high. A falling barometer indicates unsettled and possibly stormy weather.

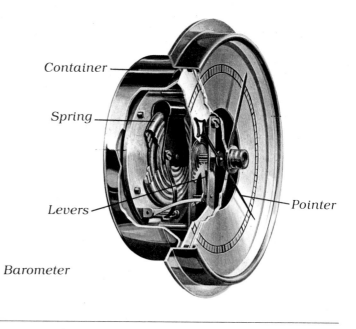

Container

Spring

Levers

Pointer

Barometer

What is the hottest temperature ever recorded on Earth?

The highest shade temperature recorded is 136°F. This was measured in the Sahara in 1922, at El Azizia in Libya, in north Africa.

Can scientists make it rain?

Drought (lack of rain) is a serious problem in many parts of the world. Scientists have tried "seeding" clouds with crystals of carbon dioxide, either from a rocket or an aircraft. The crystals act like natural ice particles in clouds, around which tiny water droplets gather to form raindrops. Another method is to release silver iodide smoke into the atmosphere. However, no scientist has yet made rain fall from a cloudless sky.

Is there anywhere on Earth where it never rains?

Records show that parts of the Atacama Desert in Chile had no rain for about 400 years. However, since 1971 some rain has fallen there, in what scientists regard as the driest place on Earth.

How cold can it get on Earth?

The Antarctic is the coldest place on Earth, with the lowest average temperatures. In 1963 at the Vostok research station Soviet scientists recorded a temperature of −128.56°F.

How are hailstones formed?

A hailstone is a small ball of ice which falls from the sky, like a raindrop. Hail is formed in thunderclouds, in which the air is rising strongly. Water droplets caught up in this air flow are swept to the cold top of the cloud where they freeze into ice balls. In this way, a hailstone can become as big as a tennis ball. A single hailstone picked up in Coffeyville, Kansas, in 1970 weighed a surprising 1.68 pounds.

Are all deserts found in places where there is little rain?

Not all deserts are in regions where rain is uncommon. Some hot deserts are rained on, but the rain is dried by hot winds as soon as it has fallen. No rivers start in deserts, but some have rivers crossing them. The Colorado and Nile rivers both flow through deserts.

What causes acid rain?

All rain is slightly acid. But air pollution from factories and fuel-burning power stations can increase the amount of chemicals in the air, making rain more acid. This acid rain may fall far away from its source and damage the environment. Trees may die, lakes may become unfit for fish to live in, and buildings may be eroded by the chemical action of the acids in the rain.

Wind erosion can create curious shapes.

How do water, wind, and heat alter the shape of the land?

Natural forces affect rock and soil, through erosion and weathering. Rain can wash away fertile topsoil and winds can blow away thin soils, leaving bare rocks on which plants cannot grow. This is erosion in action. Erosion can cause new deserts to be formed. Alternate heating and cooling of rocks can crack them into smaller pieces, to be washed away by rain and rivers. Even mountains may, over millions of years, be worn away. Rainwater can also react with minerals to dissolve rock. Such wearing away of rocks is called weathering.

What is the greenhouse effect?

The fuels we burn (in cars, houses, power stations, and factories) give off carbon dioxide gas. This builds up as a layer in the atmosphere. Heat from the Sun is reflected back from the Earth and most of it normally escapes into space. However, the thickening layer of carbon dioxide acts like glass in a greenhouse, trapping heat inside. Scientists believe that the "greenhouse effect" could, by warming the planet, change the climate in some parts of the world.

INVENTIONS

When were the first tools made?

Long before human beings had evolved, there were apelike creatures that scientists have named *Australopithecus*. They used sticks and stones as weapons. Scientists have discovered simple pebble tools made more than two million years ago.

When were the first factories started?

Stone Age people settled in places where there were plenty of stones for toolmaking. They dug holes in the ground to mine the best stone, which was flint. They traded stone tools made in "factories" with their neighbors.

How did people discover fire?

Ancient people feared fire, as animals do. A forest fire, started by lightning, sent them fleeing. Someone, somewhere, must have plucked up courage to seize a burning branch. He or she used it to start a small fire for warmth and protection against fierce animals. These first fires were kept burning constantly, for no one yet knew how to make fire.

What was a bow drill?

The oldest methods for making fire used friction: by rubbing sticks together or by striking sparks from a flint. The bow drill made firemaking simpler. It was originally an Egyptian tool, used for drilling holes. A cord twisted around a pointed stick was "bowed" backward and forward (kind of like playing a violin) so that the point of the stick twirled in a hollow. The friction produced by bowing set fire to scraps of dry grass and moss.

Who invented the wheel?

No one knows when or where the wheel was first used, but it was one of the most important of all human inventions. The wheel seems to have been discovered before 3000 B.C., probably in several different places. It may be that before they were fixed to carts and revolutionized transportation, wheels were first used by potters to turn clay pots.

Why was the waterwheel so important?

The waterwheel was the first invention that put natural forces (a river or a stream) to work in the service of people. Waterwheels were first used during the Roman Empire. The running water of a stream turned the wheel, which had paddles or blades on its rim. A simple gearing system transmitted the power to a millstone to grind corn into flour.

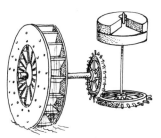

Roman water mill

Making fire with a bow drill.

Where was the world's first power station?

A Roman water mill complex at Arles in southern France was the world's first power station. There were 16 water wheels in all, providing enough power to drive 32 flour mills.

When was the wind first harnessed as a source of energy?

The first windmills were built in the Middle East around A.D. 600. Their sails looked like the blades of a lawn mower standing on end. As they turned in the wind, they also turned the drive shaft of a heavy millstone at the base of the mill. Windmills with vertical sails first appeared in Europe some 500 years later. They needed a gearing system to transmit the power to the millstone.

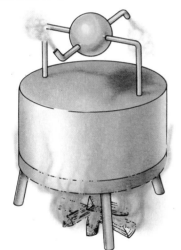

Hero's steam engine

Who invented a steam turbine as a toy?

Hero of Alexandria, a Greek who lived shortly before the birth of Jesus, was a brilliant inventor of gadgets. He made an automatic puppet theater, a toy bird with flapping wings, and even a slot machine. His steam turbine toy was a metal sphere hung between two brackets so that it could spin. It was filled with water and heated over a fire. When the water boiled, steam escaping from two jets in the sphere set it spinning on its axis. Hero had invented a simple jet engine, but since no one could think of a use for it, his gadget remained just an amusing toy.

How long have people used weighing machines?

Accurate scales or weighing machines are vital for science, and also for trade and business. The ancient Egyptians had equal arm balances much the same as are still used today. Such balances have been in use for some 7,000 years!

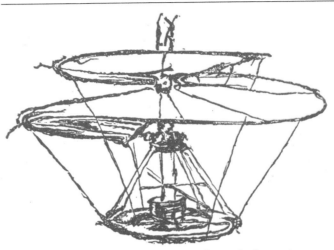

Leonardo da Vinci's design for a helicopter

Why did Leonardo's flying machine never fly?

The Italian Leonardo da Vinci, who lived between 1452 and 1519, dreamed up inventions that were centuries ahead of their time. He drew plans for a submarine, a parachute, an armored vehicle something like a tank, a helicopter, and a flying machine. His flying machine was never built, for no existing engine was able to power it. The age of light, powerful motors had yet to come.

Who was the most inventive inventor of all time?

This title probably belongs to inventor Thomas Alva Edison (1847–1931), with more than a thousand inventions to his credit. Among them were the electric light bulb, the film camera, and the phonograph (an early form of record player).

Thomas Alva Edison

Steam Age

What was the "bone digester"?

The French scientist Denis Papin was living in England in the 1670s as a friend of the famous physicist Robert Boyle. He built the world's first pressure cooker to show that steam "superheated" under pressure produced greater heat and energy. Papin demonstrated this by cooking beef bones until they were soft. He even cooked a "scientific dinner" for members of the Royal Society.

What useful device did the first pressure cooker introduce?

Papin's pressure cooker was in danger of exploding if too much pressure built up inside. He therefore devised a safety valve. When steam within the container reached a dangerously high pressure the valve was forced open. Steam escaped, pressure dropped, and the valve closed again. Papin's invention was essential if steam engines were to work safely.

What was the first steam engine used for?

In 1698 an English engineer named Thomas Savery devised "an engine for the raising of water and occasioning motion to all sorts of mill works." His engine was put to work pumping water from the shafts of tin mines in Cornwall.

How did early steam pumping engines work?

Savery's steam pump had a condenser—an iron vessel into which hot steam was passed from a boiler. Cold water was sprayed on the outside of the condenser, cooling it, and turning the steam to water. This created a partial vacuum which sucked in mine water through an inlet pipe until the valve on the pipe was shut off. Then more hot steam was let into the condenser, forcing out the waste water through a discharge pipe.

Who added a piston to his steam engine?

The pioneer of the steam piston engine was Thomas Newcomen (1663–1729). His engine had a single piston, fitted inside a cylinder. The piston began its cycle at the top of the cylinder, held in place by a counterpoised weight. Then hot steam was let into the cylinder and condensed (cooled to water), creating a vacuum. Air pressure on the head of the cylinder pushed it down to the bottom, overcoming the vacuum. The next inlet of hot steam pushed out the condensed water, which ran out through a valve at the bottom of the cylinder. The cycle then began again.

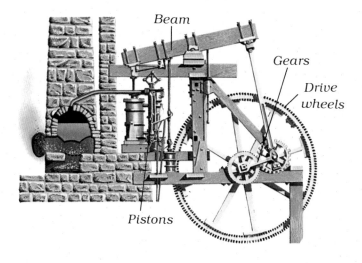

Watt's improved steam engine

Why do so many people believe that James Watt invented the steam engine, when he didn't?

The Scottish engineer James Watt (1736–1819) is said to have been inspired to improve the steam engine by watching a kettle boil. In 1764 he was trying to repair a model of a Newcomen steam engine. Realizing how inefficient this kind of steam engine was, Watt added a separate condenser to make it more powerful. He also worked out how to change the up and down motion of the beam engine into rotary motion, suitable for driving machinery. These brilliant improvements earned James Watt fame as the "father of the steam age."

Technological Marvels

Who built the first automated mill?

In the 1780s the American Oliver Evans (a pioneer of steam engines) built a mill in which grain was ground into flour entirely by machinery. The grain was delivered by wagon or barge, and raised to the top floor by a screw conveyor linked to an endless belt and bucket arrangement. Gravity provided the power from then on, as the grain fell through hoppers to the millstones. It was years ahead of its time, but few people showed much interest in Evans' mill.

When were cars first built on an assembly line?

Until 1914 cars were built one by one, as wagons had always been. A group of workers finished one car before starting on the next. Automobile maker Henry Ford changed all this by introducing the first assembly line into his factory. Cars moved along an automated conveyor system. Each part (seats, engine, wheels, and so on) was put on in turn as the conveyor moved along carrying the car bodies. Instead of taking 13 hours to build a Ford Model T car, it took only one and a half hours using the new assembly line.

Jacques Cousteau invented the Aqua-lung and mouthpiece.

What power drove the first spinning machines?

Among the first industries whose expansion began the Industrial Revolution were spinning and weaving. These tasks had always been done at home, usually with women spinning and men weaving. In 1769 (the same year that James Watt patented his improved steam engine) Richard Arkwright patented a spinning machine. But Arkwright's machine was driven by a waterwheel, not steam. The waterwheel drove a belt to spin the rollers over which cotton thread was pulled to make it fine.

Which astronomer invented a diving bell?

In 1690 Edmund Halley (of comet fame) invented a wooden diving bell. It was cone-shaped, made of wood coated with lead, and was lowered into the sea to a depth of 65 feet. Inside were Halley and four intrepid friends. Fresh air was lowered to them in barrels on the end of a rope, and this enabled Halley to stay under water for 90 minutes. Halley's bell was not the first, but it was a great advance on previous designs.

What is an Aqua-lung?

Skin divers have ventured below the sea since ancient times, but they could stay below only for as long as their breath allowed. A diver in a heavy diving suit relies on air pumped down through a hose. Not until the 1930s was self-contained diving gear invented. Divers carry air in bottles on their back and breathe through valves in their face mask. Called Aqua-lung equipment, it was developed by the French diver Jacques Cousteau.

How can frogmen dive in secret?

During World War II frogmen carried out daring underwater raids. They wore a "rebreathing" diving suit, breathing in oxygen. The oxygen passed from a cylinder to a rubber bag before being breathed in. The air the diver breathed out was purified by chemicals and returned to the bag to be used again. The great advantage of this gear was that no telltale air bubbles were released to give away the frogmen's position.

How was the *Titanic* rediscovered?

The ocean liner *Titanic* sank in 1912 after colliding with an iceberg in the North Atlantic Ocean. It was one of the greatest disasters at sea, especially as the ship was thought unsinkable and more than 1,500 passengers drowned. In 1985 the wreck of the *Titanic* was found by scientists using sonar echo sounders. It lay on the seabed at a depth of 2.5 miles. A small robot submarine, linked to its support ship by cable, was sent down to explore.

The ill-fated Titanic

How were the timbers of the *Mary Rose* preserved after being in water for 400 years?

The warship *Mary Rose*, built for King Henry VIII of England, sank in 1545 off the coast of southern England. The wreck was found in 1971 and raised in 1982. Much of the ship's timbers had been preserved in the mud. To prevent them drying out (and falling to pieces) they were first sprayed constantly with water and then soaked in a solution of sugar alcohol or polyethylene glycol. These chemicals replaced the water in the timber fibers. When freeze-dried, the timbers were almost as good as new and the restored *Mary Rose* went on view to the public at Portsmouth, England.

How does a river flood barrier work?

The river Thames in London has a huge barrier at Woolwich to prevent flooding. Four main gates, each weighing roughly 4,400 tons, and six smaller gates can be raised to form a barrier across the river. The gates would be raised if a high flood tide surged upstream from the sea, to prevent flooding of the main city.

The Thames barrier

Why would scientists build a model of a flying dinosaur?

We know that there were giant flying reptiles during the Age of Dinosaurs millions of years ago. Their fossils have been found. But no one is sure how these creatures flew. Did they flap their wings, or glide from cliffs? Scientists in the US have built a model of the largest flying dinosaur known, to see just how well a creature with a wingspan of 10 yards could fly.

What is a wind tunnel?

Wind tunnels are used by aircraft designers to test models of new planes. The model is fixed inside the tunnel, where a fan blows air over it at different speeds. Observers study how the model behaves and alter the design accordingly. Wind tunnels can also be used to see how streamlining improves the performance of cars.

What is alternative technology?

Science and technology can be expensive—too expensive for the developing countries. Alternative technology can often provide simple, cheap answers to people's problems. Take a pump for raising water from beneath the desert, for instance. A diesel-engined pump needs fuel and maintenance. It will probably wear out in four years. But a simple windmill, designed to work in dry, hot conditions, can go on pumping water for 20 years. It needs no fuel and very little maintenance.

Warfare

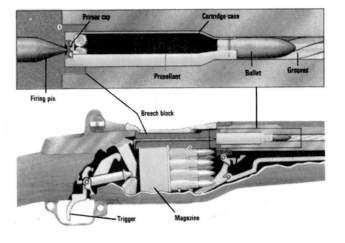

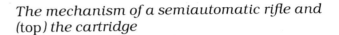

The mechanism of a semiautomatic rifle and (top) the cartridge

Who believed generals could spy on their enemies through giant lenses?

The medieval scientist Roger Bacon (a Franciscan monk) was interested in magnifying glasses. He thought Julius Caesar had used very large mirrors to see from France to England, to spy on the ancient Britons. Bacon suggested that the armies of his own day might use such mirrors "so that all being done by the enemy might be visible."

What was Greek fire?

In the 7th century the Greeks of Byzantium possessed a deadly secret weapon. Known as Greek fire, it seems to have been a petroleum-based mixture which was thrown in barrels or shot out of tubes. It caught fire spontaneously and could not be put out by water. How the Greeks made this deadly flamethrowing chemical remains a mystery. It was greatly feared by their enemies, whose wooden warships were especially vulnerable during a sea fight.

When were cannon first used in battle?

The Chinese invented gunpowder rockets, but cannon were not used for battle in Europe until the 1300s. The early guns were clumsy and fired solid cannon balls. Often their metal barrels exploded under the force of the gunpowder charge, doing more damage to their own side than to the enemy.

What was a "flash in the pan"?

The expression "a flash in the pan" means something that happens once and may not be repeated. It comes from the time when flintlock handguns were fired by means of a spark setting off a gunpowder charge. When the trigger was pulled, a piece of flint struck against a steel plate, sending a spark into the priming pan where there was a small charge of gunpowder. This "flash in the pan" set off the main charge to fire the gun.

Why do rifle bullets spin in flight?

A bullet flies farther and straighter if it is set spinning as it is fired. It acquires what scientists call "gyroscopic stability." This fact was known to archers and spear throwers long before guns were invented. The inside of a rifle barrel has spiral grooves cut into it. As the bullet speeds along the barrel, the grooves set it spinning. A gun without rifling is called a smooth-bore weapon.

Why should a rifleman beware the gun's recoil?

When a gun is fired, the exploding charge sends the bullet or shell shooting out in one direction. The charge also produces an equal force acting in the opposite direction, and this force is called recoil. An untrained rifleman can suffer a sore shoulder or be knocked backward by the recoil from a powerful rifle. Early cannon recoiled a yard or more every time they were fired.

When was the machine gun invented?

One of the first successful automatic guns was the Gatling gun, used during the American Civil War. It had up to ten barrels, which fired one after the other as a handle was turned. Some 20 years later, in 1884, came the Maxim gun which was lighter and far more deadly.

How far can the biggest guns shoot?

In 1918, during World War I, the Germans fired the so-called Paris Gun. Nicknamed Big Bertha, it had a barrel 37 yards long and fired a shell weighing 265 pounds for a distance of 72 miles. Another German gun, the K5 of World War II, had an even longer range – almost 93 miles. Today long-range missiles can far exceed the range of the longest-firing gun.

Chieftain tank

Why do tanks have caterpillar tracks?

Tanks were developed during World War I. When the first tanks crawled into battle in 1916, they ran not on wheels but on caterpillar tracks. The continuous belted track spread the weight of the tank, and so stopped it from bogging down in mud. Tracks gave better grip than ordinary wheels and allowed the tank to cross rough ground and loose sand. Caterpillar tracks were adopted for other vehicles that travel across rough ground, such as bulldozers.

How did the *Turtle* try to sink the *Eagle*?

During the Revolutionary War, in 1776, an American submarine made the first-ever underwater attack on a battleship. The submarine was the *Turtle*, designed by David Bushnell. Inside the tiny one-man craft was Ezra Lee. The *Turtle* was propelled by a hand-cranked screw. Lee managed to steer his tiny barrel-like craft beneath the British ship HMS *Eagle*, but failed to blow it up. However, Bushnell's invention was a clear warning to the world's navies; with improvements, the submarine would be an enemy to be feared.

Why did early fighter planes risk shooting off their own propellers?

Air warfare began during World War I (1914–18). The first military planes had no proper armament and pilots fired at one another with pistols. Later machine guns were fitted, but pilots of planes with front-mounted propellers faced a problem—the propeller blades were in the way. In 1915 the French pilot Roland Garros fitted steel deflector blades to the propellers and soon afterward, Anthony Fokker invented the interrupter gear. This prevented the gun from firing when a propeller blade was directly in front of the muzzle.

How does a submarine dive?

A submarine dives by flooding ballast tanks with water. The tanks are hollow spaces between the craft's inner and outer hulls. When the submarine is about to dive, valves are opened to let seawater flood the tanks. The submarine loses buoyancy and dives. To surface, water is expelled from the tanks by blowing in compressed air. This makes the submarine more buoyant, and it rises.

How do submarine crews breathe under water?

A submarine cruising just beneath the surface may take in air through breathing tubes called snorkels. A submarine in deep water cannot use a snorkel. Instead, air is made by electrolysis (passing electric current through water to separate the hydrogen and oxygen). The amount of oxygen in the air the crew breathes must be carefully controlled. "Scrubbing" devices absorb waste gases breathed out by the crew.

Why were wooden ships copper-bottomed?

Wooden ships in tropical seas were attacked by the teredo worm, or shipworm. From 1758, the British navy experimented with copper sheathing. At first there were problems because the copper reacted with the iron bolts in the hull. When copper bolts were put in use in 1783, the problem was solved.

Chemistry at Work

What makes aluminum shiny?

Aluminum is the second most widely used metal (after steel). Most aluminum is used without special finishing. But it can be made extra-smooth and shiny by treating it with an acid or alkaline solution, often at the same time as passing an electric current through it. This gives a much brighter finish than ordinary polishing.

How is iron smelted?

Iron was first made by heating iron ore in a furnace with charcoal and limestone. As the charcoal burned, the molten iron ran down and cooled into a solid mass. This "bloom" was then hammered and reheated to purify the iron. The process of melting down iron ore is called smelting.

Medieval smiths forging iron swords.

How is most modern steel produced?

Steel today is made in two ways: either by the basic oxygen process, or the electric arc process. In the first, a jet of oxygen and powdered lime is blown onto the molten metal. This can convert 420 tons of molten iron and scrap steel into pure steel in under an hour. The electric arc process uses cold scrap metal. This is melted by intense heat from an arc, or continuous spark, of electric current. It is the best method of making very high quality steels.

How was the secret of making stainless steel discovered?

Stainless steel was discovered by a scientist named Harry Brearley during World War I. He was testing steels to make gun barrels and made a batch alloyed with more chromium than before. The result was no good, so he threw the metal away. Some days later he noticed that while other scrap metal had begun to rust, the "useless" steel was still as bright as new. He had found how to make nonrusting, or stainless, steel.

The first iron bridge, at Coalbrookdale, England

How did coke help bring about the Industrial Revolution?

Abraham Darby (1677–1717) was a farmer's son turned engineer. In his iron foundry at Coalbrookdale in the English Midlands he devised a better method for smelting iron. He used coke as fuel to heat the iron ore, instead of wood charcoal which had always been used before. Coke burned at higher temperatures and added carbon to the smelting process. The iron ore melted more quickly and greater amounts of higher quality iron were produced as a result. Darby's use of coke had made one of the important steps toward the Industrial Revolution.

When was steel first made?

The Romans knew how to make steel of a kind, and metalsmiths elsewhere must have made steel by accident. During the Middle Ages, Toledo in Spain was famous for its steel swords. Large-scale steel production was not possible until the invention of an industrial steelmaking process. This was done by Sir Henry Bessemer, who invented his "converter" to make steel in 1856.

How can a tool be given a stronger cutting edge?

Adding other substances to steel can affect it in several ways. It can make it more springy, more shock resistant, and better able to withstand high temperature. Cutting or drilling tools are often tipped with steel to which molybdenum or tungsten have been added. These two alloys make steel extra tough, so the tool does not wear so rapidly.

What are so-called silver coins made from?

Precious metals such as gold and silver are too costly for making coins today. Our "silver" coins are made instead from an alloy of copper and nickel (75 percent copper and 25 percent nickel).

Why is silver used in photography?

Photographic film contains grains of silver compounds called *halides*. These are very sensitive to light, so that when light strikes them, they change chemically. When the film is developed, the light-changed ("exposed") grains have become metallic silver. The picture we see is made up of thousands of tiny specks of silver.

Why is silver used to repair human bodies?

Surgeons can repair damage to bones in the human body by inserting metal pins and plates. Silver is often used for such repairs because it does not react with the body's tissues. "Spare parts" made of silver have a long working life.

How does a zinc coat protect steel?

Zinc protects steel against corrosion. This process is known as galvanizing. Although zinc itself will corrode in damp conditions, a layer of carbonate forms, so preventing further corrosion. Should the zinc be scratched (leaving bare steel) the surrounding zinc, rather than the steel, is eaten away.

How does tungsten give us a brighter light?

Tungsten has the highest melting point of any metal at 6,116°F. It is therefore the best metal to use for the filaments inside electric light bulbs.

Which metal might you swallow to cure indigestion?

Stomach disorders such as indigestion can be caused by too much acid. Milk of magnesia is often taken to relieve indigestion. This chemical is a hydroxide of the metal magnesium. It combines with the acid and produces alkali, which reduces acid in the stomach.

Why do some hospital patients eat barium meals?

Barium sulfate is a white mineral which is not easily penetrated by X-rays. Patients having X-rays taken of their stomach and intestines swallow some barium. This makes the internal organs show up clearly on the X-ray film.

Silver wires being used to repair a broken leg.

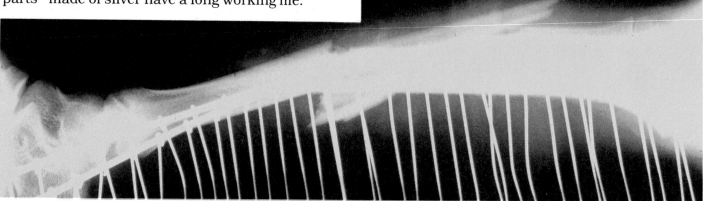

Science at Home

When were candles first used?

Candles have been in use for at least 3,000 years, and probably longer. They are mentioned in the Old Testament of the Bible, and the Romans burned candles made from flax coated with wax and pitch.

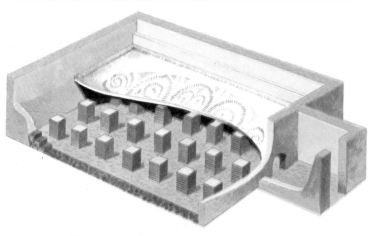

Roman hypocaust

Who enjoyed hot-air central heating 2,000 years ago?

Wealthy Romans lived in large houses with under-floor heating, known as a *hypocaust*. Slaves fed fuel onto a fire which sent hot air circulating beneath the raised floor of the house. Hot air also made its way through flues in the walls, which allowed smoke to escape. Romans living in parts of their empire far from sunny Italy (such as Britain) must have been grateful for this luxury.

What was a tinderbox?

The tinderbox was used to make fire before matches were invented. A flint was made to strike against a steel plate, producing a spark which fell into the dry "tinder" (often charred cloth). The tinder smoldered and, with some encouragement (very gentle blowing), a flame would result. Safety matches were not invented until the 1800s.

Why does a refrigerator stay cold?

When a liquid evaporates (becomes a vapor, or gas) it takes heat from its surroundings. Inside the coils of pipe in a refrigerator is a gas, such as ammonia. This gas is heated and then cooled. Cooling turns the gas into a liquid. As the liquid passes around the refrigerator pipes, it absorbs heat and becomes a gas again. Each time this cycle is repeated, the refrigerator becomes colder inside.

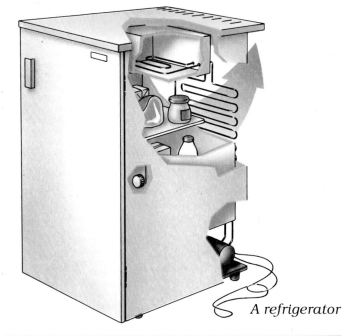

A refrigerator

How do refrigerators help to keep food fresh?

Food goes bad because of the activities of tiny bacteria. Such bacteria multiply rapidly when the temperature is higher than about 50°F. At lower temperatures the bacteria reproduce less rapidly and so food stays fresh longer.

When were frozen foods first sold?

Long ago, people realized that snow and ice kept food fresh. But until the 1800s there was no way of making ice. Before then, winter ice was cut into blocks and stored in ice houses but by the summer it had all melted. In 1834 Joseph Perkins discovered how to make ice artificially. But no stores sold ready-frozen food until the 1920s. The man who pioneered the frozen foods business was an American, Clarence Birdseye.

Which famous general was responsible for the use of glass jars to preserve food?

Ancient methods of preserving food were salting and drying. In the early 1800s the French emperor Napoleon demanded something better. Nicholas Appert thought of the answer: food boiled inside sealed jars. It stayed fresh, and Napoleon's soldiers became the first to carry bottled rations. Not until many years later did scientists understand why bottling worked. It killed the bacteria that made food decay.

One of the first canned foods, used by Sir Edmund Parry on his 1824 expedition to the Antarctic.

How many stitches a minute can a sewing machine make?

An ordinary home sewing machine can stitch at the rate of about 1,500 a minute, many times quicker than it would take to stitch the same amount by hand. Types of sewing machine were produced from about 1790 onward, but the first person to make such machines in quantity was Isaac Singer, who patented his first machine in 1851. About 2,000 varieties now exist, some of which can sew 20,000 stitches a minute.

Is it true that the first carpet cleaners blew rather than sucked?

Inventors of new household appliances in the late 1800s sometimes succeeded by trial and error. The first electric cleaners blew out a stream of air to dislodge dust from carpets. Unfortunately the dust went over everything else! In 1901 an inventor named H. C. Booth had another idea. Why not make the cleaner suck and not blow? To see if the idea worked, he lay down on the floor and tried sucking through a handkerchief. It did, and Booth built the first modern vacuum cleaner.

When did people first have zippers on their clothes?

Until the 1900s all clothing was fastened with buttons, pins, or similar fastenings. The zipper was invented in 1891 by Whitcomb Judson of the US, and improved by a Swede, Gideon Sundback, in 1913.

How do you open a can without a can opener?

Canned foods first went on sale in the 1820s. The only way to open them was with a hammer and chisel or a strong knife. Many people must have cut themselves trying—or given up and thrown the can away, still unopened. In the 1860s, an unknown inventor produced a can opener, and life in the kitchen became easier and safer.

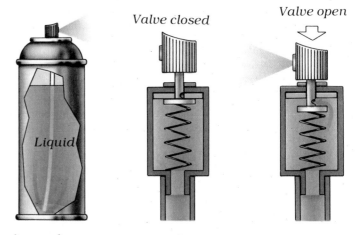

Aerosols use compressed gas.

When were aerosol sprays first used?

The aerosol spray can was invented in 1941 by an American, Lyle D. Goodhue. The container (containing paint or hairspray, for instance) also contains a propellant—a gas under pressure. The gas, mixed with the contents, sprays out when the button on the can is pressed.

Manufacturing

Will we soon be able to buy instant-print clothing?

At present, cloth is printed in a textile factory by being passed through a series of roller screens to which colored dyes have been added. It may soon be possible to buy "photocopied" designs. The colors and patterns would be transferred to the cloth using an electrostatic machine similar to a photocopier. Heat would bond the colors to the correct areas. Thousands of designs could be stored. And a computerized selection system in a store could allow a customer to choose any one, in whatever colors, and have it instantly printed on "blank" shirts, dresses, sheets, curtains, or any other kind of linen.

What was a cotton gin?

Cotton comes from the seed head of the cotton plant. The seeds must be removed and until 1793 this was done slowly by hand. Then an American named Eli Whitney patented the gin, a machine which could do the work of 50 fieldworkers. Inside the gin was a cylinder with teeth; as a handle was turned, the cylinder revolved and the teeth pulled the cotton fibers through slots. The seeds were too big to pass through the slots and fell into a box.

What were the earliest adhesives?

Some 3,000 years ago people used glues made from plants such as corn and rice, and also from the bones and horns of animals. Tree resin, tar, beeswax, egg white, and even cheese were also used as adhesives.

1. Spiked hammers turned a mixture of rags and water to a pulp. 2. The pulp was transferred to a vat. A wire screen was used to collect a thin layer which was then laid on felt. 3. These wet sheets were squeezed in a press and, 4. peeled off and hung out to dry.

How did the Egyptians cast statues in metal?

The Egyptians made statues of their pharaohs (kings) by a process known as lost-wax molding. A model was first made in wax, with every detail carefully added. It was then covered in soft clay. The clay was put in an oven to harden. As it did so, the wax melted and ran out of a drainhole in the mold, leaving inside a negative impression of the statue. Hot, molten metal was then poured into the hardened clay mold. When it had cooled, and set solid, the mold was opened or broken to reveal the finished casting.

How was paper made before the age of machines?

In the 1600s each sheet of paper was made separately, by hand. The only machines involved were trip hammers, driven by waterwheels. These ground rags mixed with water into a pulp. The pulp was then put in a vat, and a wire screen was dipped into it. The screen picked up a thin coating of pulp. It was lifted out, shaken, and laid on felt. The paper stuck to the felt, and was put in a screw press to press out the moisture. Each sheet of paper was then peeled off the felt and hung up to dry.

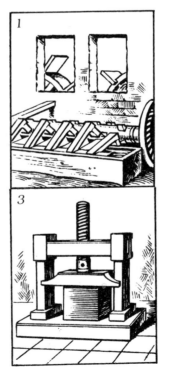

Can paper be made from synthetic fibers such as nylon?

Paper can be made from synthetic as well as natural fibers. But it costs more, because an adhesive has to be added to replace the natural stickiness of cellulose. Synthetic-fiber paper is useful, however, because it stands up well to acid and heat.

Can paper be made from any plant?

Much of the paper we use today is made from wood pulp from trees. But fibers from almost any plant can be used to make paper. Plants contain cellulose, a strong and tough material which swells up when soaked in water but retains its strength. This is what makes plant fibers suitable for paper-making.

What is a thermoset plastic?

There are two main families of plastics: *thermoplastics* (which alter shape when heated) and *thermosets*, which are resins that once formed cannot be softened and remolded. One of the first commercial plastics, Bakelite, was a thermosetting resin. It was used to make plugs and other electrical connectors.

What was the first plastic?

In 1862 a chemist named Alexander Parkes showed a new discovery at an exhibition in London. The new substance he had made was cellulose nitrate, which he called Parkesine. It was the first plastic, a tough material. Parkesine was later renamed celluloid and developed by an American, John Wesley Hyatt.

Are there natural polymers?

Starch and cellulose tissues in plants are natural polymers. Another is rubber. The monomer (the tiny molecule) in rubber is called isoprene. It polymerizes naturally inside the rubber tree, forming a sticky gum called latex. This latex is removed by "tapping" the tree; then the latex is treated and dried to form natural rubber.

What makes adhesives stick?

All substances stick together to some extent. The tendency of molecules to cling together is what literally stops the world from falling apart. Adhesives do not have to be made from naturally sticky substances. Artificial adhesives are made of chemical polymers—substances made of extra-large molecules which contain many smaller molecules called monomers. Polymers seek always to attach themselves to other polymers.

Early electrical goods were made from Bakelite. It was invented in 1907 by Leo Baekeland and was a good insulator.

Who invented the rubber raincoat?

No one could find much use for natural rubber until the 1800s. For one thing, it is affected by temperature: getting soft in hot weather and becoming stiff in cold weather. In the 1830s a Scotsman named Charles Macintosh made a laminate, or sandwich, of two sheets of cloth with rubber in between. This rubberized cloth made a good waterproof raincoat, even though on hot days, sticky rubber tended to drip out of the sandwich.

What is vulcanized rubber?

Vulcanized rubber is stronger and more stretchy than raw natural rubber. The secret of making it was discovered by an American, Charles Goodyear, using a method suggested by another American, Nathaniel Hayward. Goodyear put rubber into boiling sulfur and saw a change take place. The rubber charred, but did not burn. It emerged stronger (but still elastic) because the sulfur molecules had formed bonds with the rubber.

How is plastic foam made?

Foam plastic is a thermoplastic (polystyrene and polyurethane are examples). It is made by adding to the liquid plastic a chemical that gives off a gas when heated. The gas bubbles up through the hot plastic mixture and when the plastic cools, it has a foamy appearance.

Why does rubber stretch?

Rubber stretches because it is made of long chains of molecules, or polymers. These molecules slide easily over one another, allowing the rubber to alter its shape with ease.

When was artificial rubber invented?

Experiments to create artificial rubber were made in Germany during World War I and in other countries during the 1930s. The process was perfected in America during World War II when there was a great need for rubber, and Japanese forces controlled the rubber plantations in Southeast Asia. Artificial rubber is made from hydrocarbons (petroleum chemicals). The commonest form is known as SBR (short for styrene-butadiene rubber).

What happens inside an oil refinery?

Crude oil (a greenish-brown or black, sticky liquid) is a mixture of substances. These have many uses, but first must be separated out from the oil. This is done at a refinery by a process of distillation. Crude oil is boiled at the bottom of a container. The different substances in it vaporize (turn to gas) and rise upward. As each cools (at a different temperature) it liquefies, and each liquid is drained off at different levels of the container (called a fractionating column). The liquids are known as fractions. Those that liquefy at the highest temperature do so at the bottom of the column. Those that turn to liquid at the coolest temperatures do so at the top.

What else can coal be used for, apart from being burned?

Coal, like oil and natural gas, contains chemicals of value to the plastics and petrochemicals industries. When coal is heated to between 1,800° and 2,200°F it breaks down into four main parts: coke, coal gas, ammonia, and coal tar. Products that can be made from coal-based chemicals include dyes, drugs, insecticides, fertilizers, explosives, and solvents.

What kind of by-products do we get from oil?

Crude oil produces a number of by-products. They include gas and petrochemicals (the lightest "fractions" made during the distillation process), gasoline, kerosene, diesel oil, lubricating oil, fuel oil (used in steam turbines in power stations), and bitumen, which is the heaviest fraction.

Could we live without petrochemicals?

In today's world, we depend heavily on petrochemicals. From them are made such everyday items as plastics and nylon. About five times as much oil is used in the 1980s as was used in the 1950s. Petrochemicals have so many uses that some scientists believe we are foolish to waste such a precious and limited natural resource as oil by burning it in the engines of our cars.

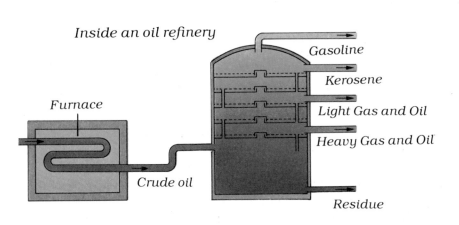

Inside an oil refinery

Furnace

Crude oil

Gasoline

Kerosene

Light Gas and Oil

Heavy Gas and Oil

Residue

Building

How were the stones of the Pyramids held together?

The ancient Egyptians used no cement to bond stones. When they built the mighty Pyramids, each stone was shaped with great care to fit precisely against its neighbor. Blocks of stone weighing as much as 120 tons were hauled into place by the muscle power of thousands of slaves.

What made the Romans such good builders?

The ancient Romans knew how to make a cement that would set hard under water—a secret not rediscovered in Europe until the 1700s. They also knew how to fire bricks and tiles in kilns. Roman builders made great use of the arch, the vault, and the dome. These enabled them to build amphitheaters, aqueducts, tunnels, bridges, walls, lighthouses, and the best roads in the world.

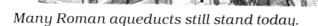

Many Roman aqueducts still stand today.

How high could medieval builders build?

The greatest buildings of the Middle Ages in Europe were the cathedrals. Builders and architects strove to outdo one another, building taller towers and higher spires. Often, because the foundations were not strong enough to support their weight, these towers collapsed. The tallest spire, at Strasbourg, rose to 465 feet—as high as a 40-story skyscraper.

How heavy is the Eiffel Tower?

The Eiffel Tower is the most famous landmark of the French capital, Paris. It was completed in 1889 and stands more than 1,000 feet high. Built of iron, it was the most futuristic construction of its time. More than 9,120 tons of iron went into the building of the Eiffel Tower.

Why were there no skyscrapers until about 100 years ago?

The taller a stone building is, the thicker must be the walls at its base, to support its enormous weight. This fact limited the height of buildings until the 1880s, when steel frameworks were tried for the first time. In 1885 the Home Insurance Building in Chicago was the first building to have walls which were not load-bearing. It was held up by a metal skeleton of girders and, though only ten stories high, was the forerunner of the skyscrapers for which American cities became famous.

Skyscrapers are built around a metal frame.

Who invented a device that made the staircase old-fashioned?

Few people want to climb more than four or five flights of stairs inside a tall building. No skyscrapers would have been built had the elevator not been invented first. There were hoists (elevators worked by pulleys) in factories. Some were driven by steam engines. In 1854 Elisha Otis demonstrated an elevator that could carry people safely. Early elevators were worked by hydraulic (water) power.

Where does the power of a pneumatic drill come from?

Drills used to break up concrete and make holes in rock are driven by compressed air. A compressor (a pump worked by a motor) supplies air under pressure through a flexible hose. The air drives a piston which in turn hammers the drill tool up and down to shatter the concrete.

How much soil can the largest earth-mover move?

The world's largest machine able to move is a dragline excavator nicknamed Big Muskie. It weighs more than 12,000 tons and its bucket can hold 220 cubic yards of earth (as much as 1,100 people crammed together!). For comparison, the bucket of an ordinary excavator you might see holds roughly 45 cubic yards.

Big Muskie, *the world's largest excavator*

How deep was the first oil well?

The Chinese were able to extract oil from below the ground 2,000 years ago. But the first modern oil well was drilled in Pennsylvania in 1859. The pioneer driller was Edwin L. Drake, who bored through 69 feet of rock to strike oil. This was 30 years before the invention of the gas-engined car. The drillers then were mainly interested in extracting kerosene, which was burned in oil lamps.

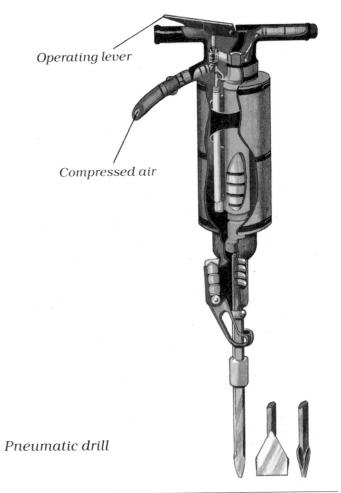

Operating lever

Compressed air

Pneumatic drill

Who first suggested the idea of a tunnel linking France with England?

A French engineer named Albert Mathieu had a novel idea for invading England in 1802. He suggested to Napoleon Bonaparte that a tunnel be dug beneath the water of the English Channel. Mathieu planned to construct an artificial island on a sandbank halfway across, so that horses could enjoy a breath of fresh air.

Which explosive made tunneling safer?

In 1866 a Swedish chemist named Alfred Nobel was working with nitroglycerine, a very unstable and dangerous explosive. By accident some nitroglycerine leaked into a box of volcanic earth called *kieselguhr* and formed a solid mass. Nobel had discovered a new explosive, which he called dynamite. The new material was much safer to transport and handle. Dynamite was used to blast rail tunnels such as the Simplon tunnel (12.3 miles long) linking Switzerland and Italy.

Farming

When did the first farmers harvest crops?

Archaeologists in Israel have found flint sickles (tools used for cutting grain) thought to be 13,000 years old. Microscopic examination of the sickle blades shows they were probably used to harvest cultivated, not wild, cereals. If this is so, farming began much earlier than was previously thought. Scientists had previously found evidence of cereal planting in Syria some 11,000 years ago.

Why did the Romans never use horses to pull plows?

In ancient Rome, oxen wearing yokes pulled heavy loads such as wagons and plows. Horses were allowed by law to pull no more than 1,100 pounds, and were never harnessed to plows. This was because horses were harnessed with a neck strap and a too-heavy load could cause the strap to choke the animal. The most efficient harness is a collar resting on the horse's shoulders, so that it does not interfere with the animal's breathing. Not until the 800s did the horse collar reach Europe (from Asia, where it seems to have been invented).

What made the horse a better work animal than the ox?

Horses cost more to feed than oxen, but there were good scientific reasons why a medieval farmer would choose a horse to pull his plow. Horse and ox were equally strong, but the horse moved 50 percent faster and could work for two hours longer. Some medieval farmers used a "horse-day" as a unit to measure how much plowing had been done. One horse-day was equal to two ox-days.

Who built the first reaping machine?

In the 1830s Cyrus Hall McCormick of the US invented a horse-drawn machine to cut grain. The mechanical reaper was followed in the 1850s by the first combine harvester.

Why do farmers grow their crops in rotation?

If the same crop is grown year after year in the same ground, the soil becomes exhausted and disease will be more likely. The Romans practiced a simple two-year rotation, letting each field in turn lie fallow (unsown) for a year. Medieval farmers introduced a three-year rotation and divided each field into three plots. Each was planted differently, in succession: wheat the first year, oats the second year, fallow the third.

During the 18th century farming techniques improved and new breeds were developed.

When did scientific farming begin?

In the 1700s the population of Europe was increasing rapidly. More food was needed, and this spurred farmers to adopt new ideas, particularly in animal breeding. The first experimental farms were started by Jethro Tull, Robert Bakewell, and others. In America, George Washington was a keen farmer and experimented with tame buffalo to see if they were better meat producers than beef cattle.

Why did the humble turnip become a vegetable of importance?

Until the farming revolution began most farm animals were killed in the autumn, because there was no winter food for them. In the Norfolk four-course system, developed by English farmers in the late 1600s, the fallow year was done away with and turnips were grown to feed cattle and sheep through the winter. The four-course rotation was wheat (first year), turnips (second year), barley (third year), clover (fourth year).

Does music improve plant performance?

A Japanese gardener claims his vegetables grow better when Beethoven is played to them. This is not a new idea. The famous 19th-century scientist Charles Darwin played the trumpet to some of his plants, to see what effect it had. Modern science has demonstrated that sound can affect plants, so musical greenhouses may well make sense in the future.

When did the first motor tractor go to work on the farm?

Gasoline engines were first used on stationary farm machinery, and only later mounted on wheels. The world's first gasoline-driven tractor was built in the US in 1892.

How did a steam plow work?

Steam power was used on farms in the 1800s to drive machinery. The steam engine usually remained stationary, although steam tractors that could move around under their own power were also used. The steam plow was hauled backward and forward across a field by long drive chains linked to one or more stationary traction engines.

When were fertilizers first used?

Farmers have always used animal manure to restore the goodness in the soil. It was not until the 1800s that they began applying chemical fertilizers. Experiments were made with saltpeter, nitrate of soda, and guano (bird droppings) from Peru. Basic slag, a waste product of the iron industry, was found to improve grassland. In 1842 John Bennet Lawes of Britain found how to produce superphosphate from rock and this was the beginning of the chemical fertilizer industry.

Why are some weed killers and insecticides harmful?

Chemicals have been used more and more by farmers to control pests and weeds. Today we know that some chemicals can cause damage to both soil and wildlife. DDT, for example, was greeted as a "wonder chemical" in the 1940s. It was a powerful weapon against the mosquito and other disease-carrying insects. But because DDT builds up in the soil its agricultural use was banned in the US in 1973.

How can farmers make pesticides stick to the right plants?

When a farmer sprays pesticide onto crops, the chemical may be later blown onto surrounding land. But if the droplets of chemical pass over an electrified plate before leaving the sprayer, they are given an electrical charge. They then stick to the next object they meet—the leaves of the crop—and spread no farther.

Why do aphids have to beware of radar traps?

Aphids (relatives of the garden greenfly and blackfly) can do great damage to potatoes and cereal crops. Particularly bad swarms are likely every three or four years. Sensitive radar can actually detect the swarms of tiny aphids so that "aphid raid warnings" can be given to farmers.

The steam plow

TRANSPORTATION

What was the earliest vehicle?

The most ancient of all vehicles is perhaps the sled. This was used in Stone Age times, and not just in snow. Putting a load (such as an animal killed for food) on a sled made it easier to drag, because the smooth wood produced less friction as it rubbed against the rough ground. Putting runners on the sled made it even easier to drag. One day someone added wheels—and made the first cart.

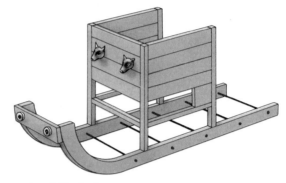

An ancient Babylonian sled

How did the Romans improve their driving?

Roman carts had either two or four wheels and were drawn by oxen or horses. Roman engineers invented the sway bar, which allowed the axle linking the front wheels of the vehicle to move from side to side. This made steering much easier and must have made Roman drivers more skillful at driving.

What was Blind Jack of Knaresborough famous for?

In the Middle Ages, England had the worst roads in Europe. Improvements began in the early 1700s, thanks to the work of roadmakers such as John Metcalf, a Yorkshireman nicknamed Blind Jack of Knaresborough. He was blind from the age of six, yet he built more than 170 miles of highways in northern England. He followed the old Roman method, laying a foundation of stone bricks and adding layers of chippings on top. Unlike the Romans, Blind Jack did not finish off the road with paving stones.

Why were roads so bad until the late 1800s?

Despite the efforts of 18th-century engineers such as John Macadam and Thomas Telford, there were no properly surfaced, all-weather roads until the motor car appeared in the 1880s. There was no demand. Few people traveled far by road, and a horse-drawn coach was the fastest means of transportation. When people began buying cars, and driving them at the unheard-of speed of 25 mph, it was quickly realized that rutted, unmade roads would have to be improved.

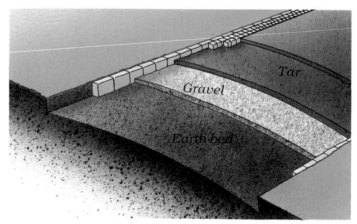

Section through a macadam road.

When was the coach invented?

The coach was invented in Hungary about 1500. Its advantages over earlier passenger-carrying wagons included being closed in against the weather. The driver rode outside on a raised seat, and four passengers sat inside. Four horses pulled the vehicle. Even so, the ride must have been very uncomfortable, since early coaches had no springs to absorb the shocks as the vehicle bumped along unmade roads.

How did Obadiah Elliot give people a smoother ride?

Steel springs on coaches were tried in the 1700s, but the biggest contribution to comfort came in 1804 when an English coachmaker named Obadiah Elliot designed the first elliptical, or oval, springs. The springs were placed between the body and the wheel axles. They absorbed the shock of all but the worst bumps and gave passengers a much smoother ride.

How did the Chinese move canal barges uphill?

The Chinese were great canal builders. To solve the problem of how to raise and lower boats between different levels they used various methods, including an inclined plane up which the boat was hauled with ropes and pulleys.

Who invented the canal lock?

A canal lock has two gates, enclosing a basin and sluices which let the water in and out. A boat moving "uphill" enters the basin by the lower gate, the gate is closed and sluices opened to allow water to pour in from the higher level. The boat floats higher as the basin fills. When the level is the same as the higher stretch of canal, the higher gate is opened and the boat moves on its way. To move "downhill" the process is reversed. The Dutch and Italians both claim to have invented locks in the 1400s. Lock design has remained basically the same since then.

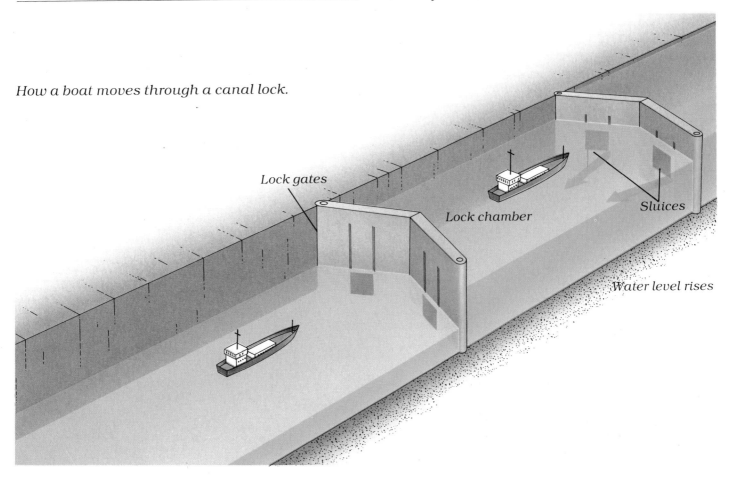

How a boat moves through a canal lock.

Lock gates

Lock chamber

Sluices

Water level rises

Railways

Did the ancient Greeks have railways?

The Greeks used wooden tracks to move ships across the isthmus of Corinth, saving a long sea journey. They had discovered that it is eight times easier to pull a load along rails than along a bumpy cart track.

Who built the first steam-driven vehicle but found no use for it?

A French soldier named Nicolas Cugnot built a carriage driven by a steam engine in 1763. It had three wheels and Cugnot thought it would be useful for hauling heavy cannon. Unfortunately, it was very slow and after a few test runs, it went out of control and somehow overturned. His superiors decided to stick with horse-drawn artillery, and Cugnot's ill-fated machine was locked up for everyone's safety.

How did the *Rocket* outstrip its rivals?

In 1829, British pioneers gathered to race their steam locomotives at the Rainhill trials. George Stephenson's *Rocket* hauled a train weighing 24 tons at a top speed of more than 35 miles per hour. The *Rocket's* three rivals (the *Novelty, Perseverance,* and *Sans Pareil*) were no match for it. Stephenson's locomotive had a multiple boiler with five tubes. This meant that more water was in contact with the heat, and so a more powerful head of steam was delivered to the pistons.

When was the world's first electric railway opened?

In 1879 a 270-yard stretch of electric railway was opened in Berlin, Germany. It was the brainchild of Werner von Siemens. Four years later, his brother Wilhelm opened an electric railway in Northern Ireland. By the 1920s electric streetcar lines were operating throughout the world.

When did diesel trains enter service?

The diesel engine was not used on railways until some 40 years after its invention. In the 1930s railways in Germany and the United States took the lead in building diesel locomotives.

What is the difference between a diesel and a diesel-electric locomotive?

A diesel locomotive has an engine resembling that in a big truck. Its pistons are linked to connecting rods that turn a crankshaft. Power for the drive wheels is taken from the crankshaft. A diesel-electric locomotive has a similar kind of engine, but uses the power to spin a generator to produce electricity. This electricity drives the traction motors that push the train along.

What was the most powerful steam locomotive ever built?

In the 1940s the American Union Pacific railroad built the Big Boy locomotives, capable of more than 6,000 horsepower and each weighing 640 tons.

Which is better: diesel or electric?

Electric trains are faster and cleaner than pure diesel trains. They also need less maintenance. However, an electric train can only use track that has been electrified. A diesel or a diesel-electric can run on any track.

Electric locomotive

Above: a funicular railway
Left: Big Boy, the most powerful steam train in the world.

Where do electric trains get their current from?

Most electric locomotives pick up current from overhead wires through an arm called a pantograph. Some trains pick up current from a third rail, laid alongside the ordinary track. The simplest locomotives operate on low-voltage DC current, but many work on high-voltage AC current which is then converted to low-voltage DC before driving the traction motors.

What kind of engine hauled the world's first subway train?

The first subway, or underground railway, opened in London in 1863. It connected the busy main-line stations of Paddington, Euston, and King's Cross. The London subway was at first a steam railway. It changed to electricity in 1890.

What is a rack railway?

A railway locomotive cannot readily climb steep hills since its wheels slip on the smooth rails. To climb mountains, a special system is needed. The first rack and pinion railway was built in 1811, but the system was not widely used until the 1870s. The train "claws" its way uphill by means of a toothed pinion, or gear wheel, which engages with the rack—a third rail with teeth cut into it. This ensures that the train cannot slip. The Mount Washington Cog Railway in New Hampshire was built in 1869 and is still working. The steepest rack railway is the Mt. Pilatus Railway in Switzerland, built in 1889, with a maximum gradient of 1 in 2.

How does a funicular railway work?

The funicular railway is a kind of cable railway used on mountains. There are twin tracks, one for uphill, the other for downhill. The two cars are linked by a cable passing up and over a driving winch in the engine room (which is at the higher end of the railway). The two cars move in unison; as one begins to go up, the other starts to descend. The weight of the downward-moving car helps to haul up the ascending car.

What keeps San Francisco's cable cars moving?

The Californian city of San Francisco is famous for the old cable cars which run up and down the city's hills. They move by gripping an endless cable which moves in a slot between the rails. The cable is released to stop the car, and gripped once more to start. The cable is kept moving by a stationary engine.

On the Road

Drais's Dandy Horse

Why did people laugh at Baron Drais and his "running machine"?

A German baron, Karl Friedrich Christian Ludwig Drais von Sauerbronn, caused a stir in 1813. He appeared in the streets of Mannheim, seated astride a two-wheeled machine which he pushed along with his feet. People laughed at his so-called running machine and were astonished that a man could keep his balance on two wheels, set one behind the other. Drais demonstrated that he could travel four times as quickly as a walker, and his machine sparked off a new craze. Similar machines, called Dandy Horses, were soon being ridden in fashionable parks all over Europe.

Who put pedals on the bicycle?

Not until the 1830s did the idea occur of using pedal power on a "running machine." A Scot named Kirkpatrick MacMillan built a bicycle with rear-wheel drive, propelled by foot levers, and some years later a German named Philippe Fischer fitted pedals to the front wheel.

What stops a bicycle from falling over?

Riding a bicycle takes practice, but most people master it without much difficulty. The early cyclists did not know why they stayed upright—although they did know that it was harder to keep their balance at slow speeds. The wheels of a bicycle have a gyroscopic effect (like a spinning top). The faster the bicycle travels, the steadier it is.

Why did early racing cycles have huge front wheels?

The first bicycles were not chain-driven. Their pedals were fixed to the front wheel. The larger the wheel, the greater the distance traveled in one revolution of the pedals. Bigger wheels gave higher speeds, and by the 1870s bicycle racers were tearing around on bikes with huge front wheels that were known as pennyfarthings.

When did the modern bicycle appear?

Several improvements in bicycle design brought about the shape we know today. The pedals were moved from the front wheels to a position between the wheels and a chain drive was added. Wire-spoke wheels, sprung saddles, gears, ball bearings and a free-wheel device were other important changes made by the 1880s. Last to be added was the pneumatic (air-filled) tire.

The modern bicycle appeared after 1880.

Who built the first internal combustion engine?

In 1863 a Frenchman named Etienne Lenoir designed an engine which burned coal gas. He used it to drive a cart. In 1864 the Austrian Siegfried Marckus built a similar engine that used gasoline vapor, and designed an electrical ignition system.

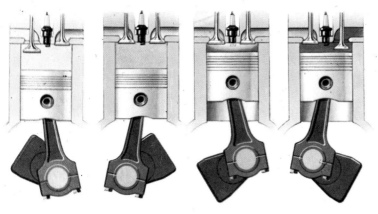

1. Induction 2. Compression 3. Power 4. Exhaust

What is meant by a four-stroke engine?

A stroke is an up or down movement of the piston. A four-stroke engine has a working cycle of four stages: induction, compression, power, and exhaust. On the induction stroke, the piston travels downward and the gasoline-air mixture is drawn in. On the compression stroke, the piston moves upward, compressing (squeezing) the mixture which is ignited by a spark from the spark plug. An explosion (combustion) takes place. The piston is sent rapidly downward by the explosion. This is the power stroke. On the exhaust stroke, the cylinder moves upward and the burned gases are pushed out through the exhaust valve.

What makes a car engine go?

The power of the car engine comes from an explosion. If gasoline is mixed with air and then ignited by a spark, it explodes. In the internal combustion engine, these explosions are controlled inside cylinders. Each explosion sends the piston inside the cylinder moving downward. The piston is connected to a series of shafts which in turn are connected to the wheels of the car.

Why do engines have more than one cylinder?

Most cars have four or six cylinders, and some have eight. A car with a single cylinder would move in a series of jerks, as each explosion happened inside the cylinder. With several cylinders the timing of the explosions can be adjusted so that they happen one after the other, very rapidly.

Who invented the rotary engine?

The rotary car engine was invented by the German engineer Felix Wankel in 1956. It has a four-stroke cycle, but a triangle-shaped rotor (or rotors) instead of pistons. As the rotor spins it converts the fuel energy directly into rotary (spinning) motion to drive the wheels. The rotary engine produces power on each of its four strokes; in a piston engine only one of the four strokes produces power.

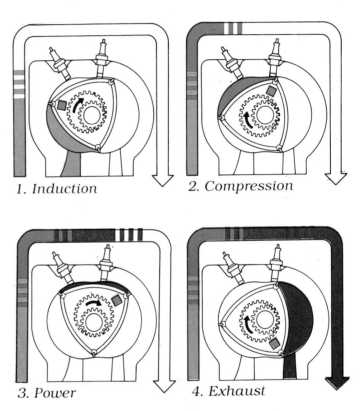

1. Induction　　*2. Compression*

3. Power　　*4. Exhaust*

In the Wankel rotary engine there is a single triangular rotor instead of multiple cylinders. This reduces vibration. The Wankel engine is not widely used except by the Japanese firm Mazda.

What makes a car engine start?

To start a car engine, the driver first switches on the ignition. This allows current to flow from the battery and the engine can come to life as the starter motor turns. This motor spins the engine, which "fires" and continues running on its own. Old-fashioned cars had starting handles, which the driver turned by hand to spin the engine.

What happens inside a carburetor?

Inside the carburetor of a car engine gasoline is mixed with air. The carburetor is set to provide the correct mixture depending on the temperature and engine speed. Air from outside the engine is cleaned by a filter before being let into the carburetor. Just the right amount of gasoline is allowed into the float chamber, and a fine spray is mixed with the inrushing air. This produces a vapor, or gas, which is taken into the cylinders in turn.

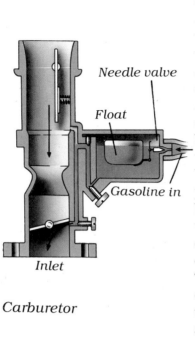

Needle valve

Float

Gasoline in

Inlet

Carburetor

What happens when the driver presses the accelerator?

Pressing the accelerator increases the amount of gasoline-air mixture entering the engine, and makes it run faster. A control called the choke makes the mixture richer in gasoline. This is necessary when starting the engine from cold.

Why do cars need a differential?

When a car (or a bus or a truck) goes around a corner, the outside wheels travel slightly farther than the inside wheels, and so have to turn faster. If the axle were in one piece, this would be impossible. So the axle is divided into two halves. These are connected to each other and to the drive shaft from the engine, by a gear arrangement known as the differential. When the car is traveling in a straight line, both wheels turn at the same speed. When turning a corner, the differential speeds up the outside wheel and slows down the inside wheel.

Karl Benz's Motorwagen, the first vehicle with a gasoline-driven engine.

How do disk brakes work?

Most modern cars have disk brakes, though another type of brake, the drum brake, is also used. Disk brakes have a metal disk which spins at the same time as the wheel. On either side of the disk are brake pads, gripped together by a caliper. When the driver's foot pushes down on the brake pedal, fluid travels from a master cylinder to "slave" cylinders at the wheels. These cylinders produce a powerful force that presses the pads against the disk and so slows down the car.

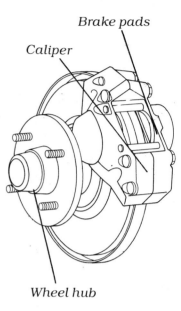

Brake pads

Caliper

Wheel hub

Disk brake

When did the first motor vehicle take to the road?

The first motor vehicle powered by a gasoline engine was a three-wheeler built in 1885 by Karl Benz, a young German engineer. His first trial run in his "horseless carriage" ended in an accident, when he drove it into a wall. The same year that Benz tested his machine, Gottlieb Daimler, working less than 62 miles away, built a motorcycle. By 1886 Daimler had produced his first car. It had a single-cylinder engine and a top speed of 18 mph.

Why are engines rated in horsepower?

The size of an engine is measured in cubic centimeters (cc). But "horsepower" is used to express the power of the engine. James Watt suggested the unit after doing experiments to see how much work a cart horse could do. A horse (or an engine) exerts 1 horsepower (hp) when it moves a load of 100 pounds a distance of 109 yards in 1 minute. Scientists today prefer to measure power in watts (named after Watt); 1 hp is equal to 745.7 watts. Electrical appliances also have power ratings in watts.

What is the difference between a diesel engine and a gasoline engine?

Unlike the gasoline engine, the diesel engine has neither an electrical ignition system nor a carburetor. Its cycle is as follows. The piston moves down as air is let into the cylinder. The compression of air by the piston moving upward produces great heat. This heat ignites the fuel (which is an oil thicker than gasoline) as it is sprayed in through a fine nozzle. The ignited fuel explodes, sending the piston down again, and on its final up stroke exhaust gases are pushed out.

Who invented the diesel engine?

The diesel engine takes its name from its inventor, Rudolf Diesel, who patented the idea in 1892. He wanted to make an engine that would burn almost any fuel. Diesel engines are widely used in trucks and other heavy vehicles, because they are cheaper to run than gasoline engines and easier to maintain. As gasoline has become more expensive, diesel-engined cars have also become popular.

Why was an engine linked to the gas main a great advance in technology?

In 1872 a German named Nikolaus Otto built a gas engine. Like a steam engine, it had a cylinder and piston. But the fuel was burned inside the piston, not in a separate furnace. Otto used gas from the gas main to drive his engine. It was a fixed engine, and he thought its main use would be in factories.

How are cat's eyes on roads kept clean?

The cat's eye, or road reflector, was invented in 1934 as a simple but effective road marker at night. The glass eyes reflect light from the headlights of oncoming vehicles. The eyes are set in a protective rubber casing. When a vehicle passes over a cat's eye, the rubber wipes the eye clean.

Above: One of the fastest road cars, the Porsche 959.

Below: Thrust 2, *holder of the land speed record.*

How fast can a car travel?

Cars fitted with rocket and jet engines can travel much faster than those with ordinary gasoline engines. The record is currently held by Richard Noble in the jet-engined *Thrust 2*, which reached a top speed of 651 mph in 1983.

Ships

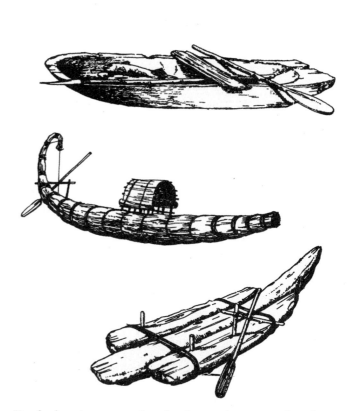

What were the first boats like?

The earliest boat was probably a floating log. Then people learned how to build rafts by lashing together logs or bundles of reeds. They hollowed out tree trunks to make canoes. The first boats were driven by paddles. Sails came later.

What made Inca sailing rafts simpler to steer?

A flat-bottomed raft is not the easiest craft to steer. Unlike a boat, it has no keel. But some scientists believe that long ago South American sailors, including the Incas of Peru, made voyages on ocean-going rafts. The secret seems to have been the use of center boards. These were rudder-like pieces of wood which could be raised and lowered through the bottom of the raft. By skillful use of these boards, a raft could be sailed against the wind, as well as with it.

Early boats were simple dugouts or made of reeds lashed together.

When did ships first have rudders?

Early ships were steered by a large oar hung over the stern. Chinese vessels were probably the first to be fitted with a rudder, and by the 1200s ships with rudders had appeared in Europe.

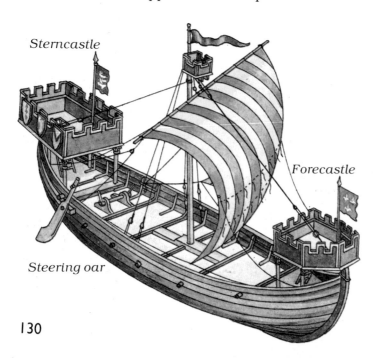

Sterncastle

Forecastle

Steering oar

Who built the first steam-driven boat?

By the late 1700s inventors in several countries were experimenting with the new power of steam to drive mechanical ships. In 1783 a French nobleman, the Marquis de Jouffroy d'Abbans, built a boat with paddles worked by a steam engine. He called it the *Pyroscaphe* (meaning "fire craft") and tested it successfully on a river.

Why are some naval ships made of wood or glass fiber?

Mines are underwater bombs, usually tethered to the seabed in the path of shipping. Special naval craft called minesweepers have the task of finding and clearing mines. Two common types of mine are acoustic mines (set to explode at the sound of a ship's engines) and magnetic mines (which explode when anything metallic is in range). For protection against magnetic mines, minesweepers are made from nonmagnetic materials, such as wood, plastic, or glass fiber.

How did Archimedes' idea help ships to go faster?

The Greek scientist Archimedes invented a water-pumping device by using the principle of the screw. The idea of using a screw propeller for ships had been thought of in the 1750s, before there were steam engines capable of driving such a device. The American John Fitch experimented with a screw-driven craft, and in 1828 an Austrian named Joseph Ressel tested a small steamboat with a screw but was forced to give up when the boiler exploded. The screw was proved workable in the 1830s, by the Swedish-American John Ericsson, and by an English farmer-turned-inventor, Francis Pettit Smith, who built a screw-driven ship which he called the *Archimedes.*

Why was the paddlewheel overtaken by the screw propeller?

Most early steamships had paddlewheels. Paddlewheels were fine in calm water, but much less effective in a rough sea. If the ship rolled, the wheel on one side lifted clear of the water, causing the engine to "race," but producing no power whatsoever. In the 1830s the screw propeller was invented. Though smaller than the paddlewheel, the propeller acts on a much greater volume of water and so has a more powerful effect. This was clearly demonstrated in 1842 when the screw-propelled *Rattler* pulled the paddle steamer *Alecto* backward in a trial "tug of war" contest.

Which was the only ship to have screws, paddles, *and* sails?

In 1858 the British engineer Isambard Kingdom Brunel built the world's largest ship. Named the *Great Eastern*, it was a giant of its time: more than 22,800 tons and 231 yards long. The *Great Eastern* had a 26-foot propeller, twin 62-foot paddlewheels, five funnels, and six masts carrying sails (in case the engines broke down). Even so it was a failure: no port was ready to handle such a huge liner, and the *Great Eastern* ended its days as a cable-layer.

Brunel's unsuccessful Great Eastern

Who invented the steam turbine?

The high-speed steam engine was made possible by Sir Charles Parsons, who invented the turbine in 1884. Steam was passed through the blades of a series of spinning rotors, which converted the steam's energy into fast circular motion. Parsons also saw the possibility for high-speed ships. His steam turbine-powered launch *Turbinia* startled naval experts on its first demonstration in 1894, reaching a speed of almost 40 mph.

Why do cruise ships give passengers a smooth voyage even in rough seas?

Modern luxury liners, such as the *Queen Elizabeth 2*, have gyroscopes controlling stabilizer fins on the hull. These fins can reduce a roll of 20 degrees to one of only three degrees (hardly noticeable). Cargo ships keep stable in heavy seas by pumping water from one side of the ship to the other. If the vessel rolls one way, water runs through a pipe to a tank on the opposite side, correcting the ship's balance.

Which ship was designed to stand on end?

The research ship *FLIP* (Floating Instrument Platform) was built in 1962 as an underwater laboratory. By flooding tanks in its bows, the ship could flip itself on end, so that only its stern remained above water. Scientists in the bows were then able to carry out underwater research on the marine life passing around them.

A hydrofoil

Why can a hydrofoil travel faster than an ordinary speedboat?

A hydrofoil has special legs, or foils, beneath its hull. When motionless, the hydrofoil floats low in the water like a normal craft. But with speed it lifts up on its foils, so that it skims over the surface of the water. This reduces the friction between the hull and the water and means the hydrofoil can travel at high speed—more than 68 mph.

What keeps a Hovercraft from sinking?

Hovercraft, or air-cushion vehicles, ride on a cushion of air. The Hovercraft has fans which blow air downward. This air is trapped inside a flexible "skirt," making a "cushion" on which the craft rides. Air screw propellers drive the Hovercraft along, skimming over land or water. The fastest speed reached by a Hovercraft is 102 mph.

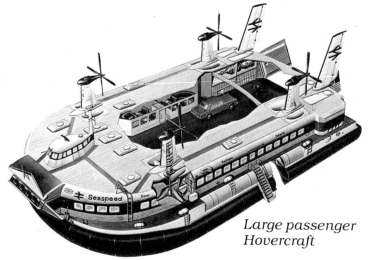

Large passenger Hovercraft

Which ships are driven by nuclear engines?

Nuclear power is used in submarines and has also been tried in surface ships. The first nuclear vessel was the US submarine *Nautilus* (1955). The Russians built a nuclear-powered icebreaker, the *Lenin*, in 1959. It can keep working all winter long without refueling. There have been experiments with nuclear-powered cargo ships, but the nuclear reactor and its protective shielding take up valuable cargo space so any future nuclear ships would have to be very large to be economical.

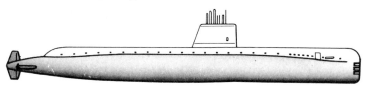

Nautilus, the first nuclear vessel

What is the world's largest ship?

Oil tankers are by far the largest ships afloat today. The largest was the *Seawise Giant* (1976), which was over 500 yards long and 555,822 deadweight tons.

How is the tonnage of a ship calculated?

There are three ways of measuring the weight of a ship. Bulk carriers, such as oil tankers, are measured in *deadweight* tonnage (the total of cargo, crew, fuel without the ship's structure). Cargo and passenger ships are measured in *gross tonnage* (internal volume). Warships are measured by *displacement* (the ship's weight plus the weight of everything on board).

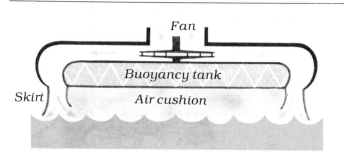

The craft floats on an air cushion contained by a rubber skirt.

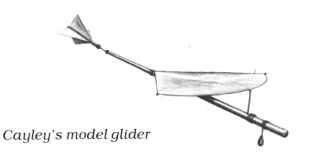

Cayley's model glider

Aviation

What was "Montgolfier air"?

In 1783 the Montgolfier brothers surprised everyone by launching the first balloons inflated with hot air. The balloons flew because hot air expands, becoming less dense than the surrounding air. But rumors spread that the brothers made their balloons work by using a mysterious "air," an unknown gas produced by burning. One report claimed that the brothers burned old shoes and rotten meat to produce their "rising gas"!

When did the first hydrogen balloon fly?

In August 1783, soon after the Montgolfiers had flown their first hot-air balloon, J.A.C. Charles and the Robert brothers flew a balloon filled with hydrogen. It was small (13 feet across) but making the hydrogen gas to fill it took many hours. To make enough gas, 498 pounds of sulfuric acid and 992 pounds of iron filings were needed. The balloon soared more than 3,300 feet above Paris and landed over 12 miles away.

Who were the first people to fly?

Over the centuries many brave but misguided experimenters have tried to fly. We know of nobody who succeeded before November 21, 1783, when two men, Pilâtre de Rozier and the Marquis d'Arlandes, flew in a Montgolfier hot-air balloon above Paris. Their historic flight lasted 25 minutes.

How is a gas balloon controlled in flight?

As a balloon rises, the air pressure around it gradually drops. In theory, the balloon should reach a certain height and stay there. But in fact, the balloon rises so quickly that it overshoots this point. As the gas inside expands in the thinning air, some of it escapes through the balloon's neck. The balloon begins to sink, but the pilot can stop it by throwing out ballast (such as bags of sand) to lighten the balloon and make it rise again.

Who sent his coachman up in a glider?

Sir George Cayley was a British scientist who worked out the forces involved in heavier-than-air flight. In 1804 he flew a small model glider, but did no further work until, in 1853, he built a full-sized craft. Then he ordered his terrified coachman to try the glider out. Cayley had proved that flight was possible, but he never repeated the experiment.

Why could kite flying have brought forward the invention of the airplane?

Kite flying is an ancient pastime, particularly in the Far East. The four forces that act on an airplane in flight (lift, drag, weight, and thrust) also act on a kite. A man-carrying kite could have been flown in the Middle Ages. But scientists, including Leonardo da Vinci, were convinced that imitating birds was the way to fly. They tried to build machines with flapping wings, not realizing that human muscles are not powerful enough to make such machines work.

Early human attempts at flight mimicked birds.

Why do aircraft have curved wings?

The wing (or airfoil) of an aircraft keeps it in the air by generating *lift*. To get as much lift as possible, the wing is curved at the top and flat underneath. Air flows faster over the top than underneath because it has farther to travel. This means that the air pressure above the wing is less than the pressure beneath it. The suction effect created by this lifts the wing. More lift comes from the slower air pushing upward as it flows beneath the flat wing surface.

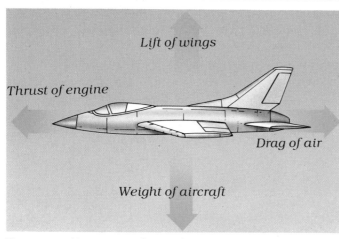

Forces acting on a plane during flight

What gives an aircraft its thrust?

Lift, thrust, drag, and weight are the four forces which act on an aircraft. Lift from the wings helps to overcome the force of gravity pushing the craft back to earth. To generate lift, the aircraft must move through the air at speed. To do this it needs thrust, supplied either by a propeller or a jet stream from an engine. For the aircraft to fly forward the thrust must be strong enough to overcome the drag (air resistance).

Can aircraft fly without engines?

A glider is an airplane which flies without an engine. It stays aloft by diving at a very flat angle, so that air flows over its wings fast enough to maintain lift. For extra lift, gliders have very long wings. Their light, streamlined bodies reduce weight and drag. A glider launched from a towing aircraft descends very slowly. If the pilot finds a rising current of warm air (called a thermal), the glider can circle within it.

How did Otto Lilienthal fly?

The German Otto Lilienthal built and flew batlike hang gliders, which he controlled by swinging his body. He made more than 2,000 flights before being killed while gliding in 1896.

Otto Lilienthal's glider

Why did Orville Wright lie on his stomach during the first airplane flight?

In 1903 the Wright brothers, Wilbur and Orville, made the first sustained flight in a powered craft when their *Flyer 1* took to the air on December 17, 1903. It had a homemade gasoline engine set on the starboard (right-hand) wing. To keep the plane stable, the pilot had to lie on his stomach on the port (left-hand) wing.

Orville Wright takes to the air in Flyer 1.

Did people parachute-jump in the Middle Ages?

People wearing parachutes may well have leapt from cliffs or towers in the 1400s. Drawings made at this time show devices which look much like parachutes. One from Siena, Italy, shows a cone-shaped canopy fastened to a wooden base, with the parachutist hanging underneath.

Why did airship-building stop in the 1930s?

The great airships of the early 1930s were huge and impressive. They cruised above the oceans carrying passengers in luxury. But they had a serious drawback. Their gas bags were filled with hydrogen, which catches fire easily. Many airships were lost in accidents. In 1937 the giant *Hindenburg* caught fire while mooring after a flight and 37 people were killed. This ended the airship's career as a rival to the airplane.

Which gas do modern airships use?

The airship has made a comeback in recent years, both for pleasure flights and as a military craft. It is ideal for ocean patrols because it can stay in the air for many hours. Today's airships are filled with helium gas. This is not as light as hydrogen, but is much safer to use because it will not burn.

Why are propeller-driven planes slower than jets?

Jets are faster than propeller planes for two reasons. First, jet engines develop greater thrust. Second, at speeds of over 500 mph the blade tips of a spinning propeller are moving so fast (near the speed of sound) that they no longer "bite" into the air properly.

What is a variable-pitch propeller?

A propeller blade has four different positions. It can be set to fine pitch (for takeoff), coarse pitch (for cruising), feathered (when the engine is stopped, so that the propeller stops turning), and reverse pitch (to brake the aircraft).

The first jet to fly, the Heinkel He-178.

The Hindenburg *crash, a tragic end to the great airship era.*

When did jets first fly?

Piston engines were found not to work well at high altitude where the air is thin, nor at very high speeds. A new type of engine was needed. As early as 1930 a British air force officer named Frank Whittle had patented a jet engine design, but the first jet plane to fly was built in Germany. This was the Heinkel He-178 which was tested in 1939.

What happens in a jet engine?

In a simple jet engine, air is sucked in at the front through compressors (which are short blades on a spinning turbine shaft). The air passes into a combustion chamber where the fuel is burned. The hot exhaust gases produce the thrust that drives the plane forward.

What is a turbofan engine?

Most modern airliners have turbofan engines. These have longer blades at the front of the compressor than in a simple jet engine. The blades act as a fan, pushing in extra air which flows around (not through) the combustion chamber. The result is more thrust, but less noise.

Why are swing-wing planes so called?

The best shape for a very fast aircraft is a thin, swept-back "delta" wing, which minimizes drag. But such designs do not handle well at low speeds. In a swing-wing aircraft, the wings are set at right angles to the body for slow flight (takeoff and landing). When high speed is required, the wings are moved to a swept-back position.

Why can a helicopter fly backward?

A helicopter's rotor blades act as both wings and propellers. To hover, or to fly upward, the blades are kept flat. To fly forward, the blades are tilted forward so that they "bite" into the air. To move backward, the rotor blades are tilted toward the tail.

Retracting undercarriage

Pratt and Whitney TF 30-412 turbofan engines

Upward folding radome

Retractable air-refueling probe

Fuel tanks

Wing pivot mounting

Collision beacon

Grumman F-14 Tomcat

How does a jump jet hover in midair?

The first jet able to rise straight into the air was the Harrier. It has four swiveling nozzles which direct exhaust gases from the jet engines. When the nozzles point down, the Harrier takes off upward, or hovers in midair. To fly forward, the nozzles are swiveled until they point backward.

Have propeller-driven airliners had their day?

All airliners were propeller-driven until the 1950s, when the Comet and the Boeing 707 introduced jet travel. For a time it seemed that all airliners would be jets, but designers are now looking again at the propeller. New technology makes it possible to build propeller-driven turboprop planes that are not much slower than jets, but which use less fuel and make less noise.

What is a Mach number?

The speed of a jet aircraft is sometimes measured not in mph but in Mach numbers. Mach 1 is the speed of sound at sea level. Mach 2 is twice the speed of sound, and so on. The first plane to exceed Mach 1 and break the so-called sound barrier was the Bell X-1 in 1947. Ernst Mach (1838–1916) was an Austrian physicist who did research into the speed at which sound travels.

What is the world's fastest aircraft?

In 1955 North American Aviation built the X-15 rocket plane. It was powered by a rocket motor generating a thrust of 57,000 pounds. The X-15 had a top speed of 4,534 mph and reached a height of 67.08 miles. It was used to carry out experiments to prepare pilots for the challenge of flying in space.

The fastest plane in the world, the North American X-15

Spaceflight

A huge Saturn V rocket blasts off.

How fast must spacecraft travel to escape the Earth's gravity?

To break away from the Earth's gravity and fly into space, a spacecraft must travel at 7 miles per second (roughly 25,000 mph). To reach the other planets, even higher speed is necessary to escape the Earth's gravity.

When does a rocket break free from Earth's gravity completely?

The gravitational pull of the Earth lessens very slowly as a craft moves into space. At 93 miles, gravity is just one hundredth less than on the Earth. At 1,550 miles, it is half as great, and at 62,000 miles, one twentieth. A spacecraft must travel millions of miles away from the Earth before Earth's gravity has no effect on it. Other bodies, such as the Moon, also exert some gravitational pull on the rocket.

What makes rockets the best engines for spaceflight?

The rocket works well in space. It needs no air (unlike a jet engine); indeed, air slows it down. Most rocket engines get their thrust from the reaction between a fuel such as liquid hydrogen and an oxidant (liquid oxygen), which allows the fuel to burn.

How many people have stood on the Moon?

In 1969 *Apollo 11* made the historic first manned landing on the Moon. From 1969 to 1972 the Americans sent seven Apollo missions to the Moon. One mission, *Apollo 13*, failed to make a landing but returned safely after an explosion on board the spacecraft. The other six missions succeeded, each landing two astronauts. So in all, 12 astronauts have stood on the Moon.

What was the first real space rocket?

The first rocket which could fly fast enough and high enough to enter space was the German V2 missile. It was first fired in October 1942, flying a distance of 125 miles and landing within 2.5 miles of its target. After World War II the Americans and Russians used captured V2s to help start their spaceflight and missile programs.

How is rocket thrust measured?

The correct unit used to measure force is the newton. But it is simpler to think of thrust in terms of weight. A rocket weighing 120 tons needs a thrust of 120 tons to lift it. It will not rise immediately; it hovers until its weight decreases as the fuel is burned. Then it accelerates upward. The thrust (which remains constant while the engines are firing) gets steadily greater than the weight (which grows less as the fuel is used up). So the rocket travels faster and faster.

How much useful weight can a rocket lift into space?

A rocket carries a small load compared to its total weight. The Saturn Moon rocket, for example, weighed well over 3,300 tons on the launch pad, but almost 2,860 tons of this weight was fuel. It could lift a payload of 105 tons into Earth orbit and send a spacecraft weighing almost 55 tons to the Moon. The Saturn was last launched in 1973. It remained the biggest rocket ever fired until the Russians launched their Energia rocket in the late 1980s.

What is an ELV?

An ELV is an Expendable Launch Vehicle (a rocket that can be used only once). Examples are the European Ariane rocket and China's Long March rocket. The Americans decided to replace ELVs with the reusable space shuttle. But the 1986 accident that destroyed the *Challenger* spacecraft halted the shuttle program. Old-fashioned Titan ELVs had to be built to fill the gap until the shuttle *Discovery* was successfully launched in October 1988.

Why do deep-space probes need nuclear batteries?

Many satellites and spacecraft make electricity by using solar cell batteries to convert the energy in sunlight. But beyond Jupiter, the Sun's light is not strong enough to power solar batteries. Tiny nuclear generators must be used instead.

When did spacecraft first land on Mars?

Two Viking spacecraft visited the planet Mars in 1970–76. The craft orbited the planet, and robot landers flew down to investigate the surface. The landers took samples of the Martian soil and sent data and TV pictures back to Earth. In 1988 the Russians launched the latest Mars-bound spacecraft. They planned to land robot probes on the Martian moon Phobos but the mission was unsuccessful.

The planned HOTOL space plane

Will passengers in the 1990s travel from London to Australia in less than two hours?

Imagine a plane flying ten times as fast as *Concorde*! This could become a reality if craft like HOTOL are built. HOTOL (short for Horizontal Take-Off and Landing) is a planned space plane. It would fly into space under its own power, cruise through the upper atmosphere, and come in to land at an airport, like an airliner. HOTOL would have new "hybrid" engines that suck in air during atmospheric flight and switch to burn liquid oxygen from its own fuel tanks while in space. It could launch satellites very cheaply.

Will people ever fly to the stars?

Journeys to the stars are unlikely because of the vast distances to be covered. The fastest present-day rockets reach less than 0.005 percent of the speed of light. A speed of at least 10 percent light-speed would be needed to make a star voyage in less than 100 years.

Could nuclear explosions take space voyagers to distant stars?

A British plan for a futuristic starship, known as Project Daedalus, suggested using a nuclear pulse rocket which would produce 250 controlled atomic explosions a minute. The rocket would travel far faster than any spacecraft of today. Yet it would still take 50 years to reach the nearest star.

Communications

What was an optical telegraph?

One of the first systems for sending messages quickly over long distances was the Chappé semaphore—an optical telegraph. It used a series of signal poles, with arms that moved to different positions to represent the letters of the alphabet. The poles were set up at intervals of about 6 miles, and lights were fitted to the arms for night work. Observers (equipped with telescopes) manned each pole and relayed the signals. They could transmit a message over 125 miles in two minutes. The first Chappé semaphore was set up in France in 1794.

How did Morse invent his code?

Morse knew that a magnetic needle swinging freely would move when a wire carrying an electric current was brought near it. He made a machine in which electric current was supplied by a battery. When switched on, an electromagnet caused a pencil to mark a moving strip of paper. Long or short taps on the key controlling the current made long or short marks on the paper. Morse invented his code using combinations of long and short dashes for each letter of the alphabet. It was this simple code that made Morse's telegraph system so successful.

Which scientists' work made radio possible?

In 1864 the British physicist James Clerk Maxwell predicted that electromagnetic waves existed. In the 1880s a German, Heinrich Hertz, showed that electricity could produce electromagnetic waves when high-voltage current jumped across a gap. It was possible that the waves could act as "carriers" for messages in the form of electrical signals. Neither Maxwell nor Hertz lived long enough to see radio broadcasting become a reality, but their work had made it possible.

Who developed the electric telegraph?

In 1839 the first commercially successful electric telegraph was set up in England by Cooke and Wheatstone. But the system which succeeded beyond all others was the one developed by the American Samuel Morse. It began working in 1844. The first line operating his system ran from Washington to Baltimore.

When was the first telegraph message sent across the Atlantic?

In 1856 British and American ships laid a submarine telegraph cable across the bed of the Atlantic Ocean. The first message was sent in 1858, but soon afterward the cable broke. Another cable was successfully laid by Brunel's huge *Great Eastern* in 1866.

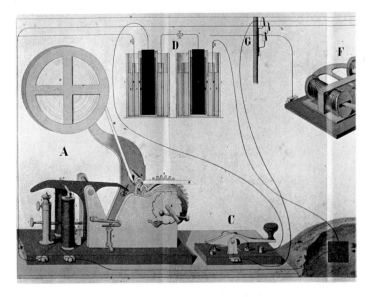

Samuel Morse's original telegraph machine

What message did Marconi transmit across the Atlantic in 1901?

Guglielmo Marconi, an Italian engineer, developed the idea of wireless telegraphy—sending messages in Morse code by radio. The Morse signals were produced by a series of electromagnetic shock waves. The first message sent across the Atlantic Ocean by Marconi consisted of a single letter – S – in Morse code.

How do sounds from a broadcasting studio reach a radio receiver?

Microphones change the sounds into electrical signals. These signals are combined with a radio carrier wave and transmitted from a tall antenna. The wave is picked up by the antenna inside a radio set, and circuits in the receiver separate the sound signals from the carrier wave. A loudspeaker changes the electrical signals back to the same sounds as were picked up by the studio microphones.

Muybridge's photo of a galloping horse

Who invented the telephone?

People knew that it was possible to send speech along a wire as early as the 1600s. Two cans linked by a length of string will show you how. But the modern telephone was first demonstrated by Alexander Graham Bell in 1876. His equipment used two electromagnets which picked up vibrations in a thin sheet of iron (the diaphragm). The vibrations were caused by the sound waves from a person speaking. This principle—the changing of sound waves into electrical signals—is the basis of all telephony.

How many calls can a telephone cable carry?

By using the technology called fiber optics, speech sound can be changed into pulses of laser light and sent along very thin glass tubes. Fiber optic cables can carry far more calls at once than an ordinary telephone wire cable—up to 40,000 conversations at a time.

Who took pictures that looked as if they were moving?

The first cameras needed a very long exposure of the photographic plate—as long as 15 minutes for one picture. To make moving pictures, film must be exposed much faster, at around 16 frames (or exposures) a second. In 1877 Eadweard Muybridge set up 12 cameras alongside a racetrack to settle a bet. A horse's owner wanted to know if his horse lifted all four legs at once while galloping. Muybridge's cameras proved that it did. The horse triggered each camera as it galloped by. Mounting the still pictures on a moving wheel and then projecting them with a magic lantern produced a moving picture.

What was a kinetograph?

The kinetograph was an early movie camera invented in 1888 by Thomas Edison. He could see no future in making moving pictures and could not imagine people wanting to watch films. A reel of the newly invented celluloid film was drawn past an opening to be exposed one frame at a time. The developed film was then run through a peep-show booth.

The Lumière brothers pioneered outdoor filming.

Who took movie cameras out of the studio?

In France, the Lumière brothers pioneered outdoor filming in the 1890s. Their cameras (in which the film reel was turned by a handle) were light enough to carry. They also reduced the speed at which film was exposed to 16 frames a second rather than the 46 frames a second used by Edison. This saved film and reduced flickering.

How was sound added to films?

As early as 1912, Edison made a film with synchronized singing and dancing. But the sound track was on a record. In the early 1920s, it was discovered how to change sound signals into light signals which were recorded on the same strip of films as the pictures.

Special effects such as stop-motion photography brought King Kong to life.

How are screen monsters brought to life?

One of the tricks used by moviemakers is stop-motion filming, which makes models appear to move. The model is placed in position and filmed for an instant. Then the camera stops and the model is moved slightly. When the film runs at normal speed, the monster "comes to life."

Whose mechanical television system was overtaken by electronics?

In 1926 John Logie Baird demonstrated television using "scanning disks." The disks had holes in them, through which light passed to a photoelectric cell. The cell gave off a pulsing electric current corresponding to the light it received. The current transmitted the signals to a second disk. When this disk was set spinning at the same speed as the first disk, the picture was reproduced. Baird's system was overtaken by a rival electronic system based on the cathode ray tube. This was used to broadcast the first public television service by the British Broadcasting Corporation in 1936.

How were television pictures first sent across the Atlantic?

In 1962 the Telstar communications satellite relayed TV pictures between North America and Europe for the first time. A network of communications satellites now orbits the Earth to provide world-wide live television coverage.

Why is a TV picture made up of lines and dots?

A TV camera records what it sees on an electrically charged plate. An electron beam sweeps across the plate in a series of lines, producing electrical signals that contain all the parts that make up the picture. These signals are carried on a radio wave from the transmitter to the antenna of your TV set. There the signals are separated from the carrier wave. Inside the TV tube is a "gun" that fires a beam of electrons at the screen causing a spot of light. The signals it receives vary the strength of this beam, and therefore the brightness of the spot. The beam sweeps backward and forward (just like the beam inside the TV camera) to produce lines of spots, each of different brightness. Because the lines are so close together, we cannot see them unless we look very closely.

Why are there mirrors inside a TV camera?

The color television camera contains tinted mirrors called *dichroic* mirrors. They split up the light entering the lens into three colors: green, red, and blue. Each of these is scanned separately and then combined into a signal sent along a cable to the transmitter. Inside your TV set the three colors are again separated and appear as tiny phosphor spots glowing green, red, or blue on the screen. Together they reproduce the original color picture.

When were video recordings first made?

Copies of TV programs had to be kept on film until the invention of videotape recording in the 1950s. The tape stores the image as a sequence of magnetic signals. Videotape made possible the "instant replay" of sports events. VCRs (video cassette recorders) became popular in the 1970s.

WHO?

Who built a steam-powered airplane?

Clement Ader of France built a flying machine, the Eole, in 1890. It had a 20-horsepower steam engine and managed a brief hop.

Who discovered oxygen?

Oxygen was discovered in 1774 by Joseph Priestley of Britain (a chemist and clergyman). He obtained oxygen by heating mercuric oxide.

Who invented the flushing toilet?

The flushing toilet, or water closet, was "reinvented" by Joseph Bramah of Britain in the 1770s. Such conveniences had been tried several times before, but had never caught on because piped water and drains were seldom available.

Who was Vladimir Zworykin?

This Russian-born engineer became an American citizen. He was one of the pioneers of electronic television, working for the Radio Corporation of America (RCA) from the 1930s.

Who was the first woman to travel in space?

This honor belongs to the Soviet cosmonaut Valentina Tereshkova (born 1937). In 1963 she made 48 orbits of the Earth in the *Vostok 6* spacecraft.

Who used wheelbarrows with sails?

The Chinese wheelbarrow differs from the Western version. It has a bigger wheel, set beneath the load rather than in front. The Chinese used barrows drawn by mules to carry passengers and also fitted small sails in order to make heavy barrows easier to push.

Who is the most famous woman scientist?

Marie Curie (1867–1934) won two Nobel prizes for physics, for discovering radioactivity and the element radium.

Who were Jeremiah Chubb and Linus Yale?

Both invented famous locks. Chubb's lock of the 1820s would (it was claimed) defeat any burglar. In the 1850s Yale introduced mass-production of locks, and in 1861 he invented the cylinder lock named after him.

Who made the first artificial dye?

Until the 1800s all dyes were made from plant or animal products. A British chemist, William Perkins, accidentally made a purple dye from coal tar. He called it "mauveine" and began manufacturing it in 1858. It was the first artificial dye.

Who invented an exploding apron?

In 1845 a German chemist named Christian Schonbein spilled onto his cotton apron a mixture of nitric acid and sulfuric acid. He hung up the apron to dry, whereupon it exploded. He had discovered a new explosive: guncotton, or nitrocellulose.

Who was the Wizard of Menlo Park?

People called Thomas Alva Edison (1847–1931) a wizard because of his brilliant inventions. His laboratory was at Menlo Park in New Jersey.

Who built the first mechanical typesetter?

In the 1880s printing was transformed by the Linotype machine, invented by Ottmar Mergenthaler, a German watchmaker who had emigrated to America. The operator sat at a keyboard, composing lines of type which were cast in hot metal ready for use on the printing press.

Who invented the aileron, for controlling airplanes in flight?

The Wright brothers controlled their airplanes by warping (twisting) the wing by means of wires. A better method was invented by Louis Blériot of France. This was the aileron, a movable section on the rear edge of the wing. All aircraft today have ailerons.

Who was the brains behind the first computer?

The code-breaking computer Colossus was built during World War II. Many of the programming techniques that made this, and later computers, possible were developed by the British mathematician Alan Turing (1912–1954).

Who put lead in gasoline and gas in refrigerators?

Thomas Midgley (1889–1944) of the US discovered that lead added to gasoline made car engines run more smoothly. Leaded gasoline went on sale in 1923. (We now know that lead pollutes the air, and cars are switching to safer, lead-free gasoline.) Midgley also pioneered the use of freon, a gas safe to use in refrigerators, freezers, and air-conditioning systems.

Who built the first successful helicopter?

Although other designs (such as the German FW-61) flew before it, the VS-300 helicopter (1939) was the forerunner of the modern helicopter. It was designed by Igor Sikorsky, a Russian who lived in the US.

Who were the first people to use paper?

The Chinese Imperial Workshops announced the first use of paper in A.D. 105. The Chinese went on to develop printing from wooden blocks.

Who built a submarine propelled by oars?

A Dutchman, Cornelius van Drebbel, built a wooden submarine in 1620. Driven by oars, it successfully crossed the river Thames in London.

Who tested a rocket-propelled sled?

In 1954 Colonel John Stapp of the US reached a speed of 632 mph on a sled. The sled ran on rails, propelled by nine rockets. Stapp's ride was an experiment to find out how acceleration and deceleration might affect pilots and astronauts. When slowing down, he experienced 40g (40 times normal gravity) and was blinded for several weeks.

Who was Octave Chanute?

Chanute (1832–1910) was an aviation pioneer. He was French but lived in America, where he carried out some 2,000 glider flights in the 1890s. He wrote letters to Orville and Wilbur Wright, exchanging ideas with them. His experiments with gliders helped the Wright brothers work out their design for an airplane.

Who began the study of geology?

The scientist who did most to found modern geology was James Lyell (1797–1875). He believed the Earth had been changed by weather, sea, and earth movements—and was still being changed. Charles Darwin took Lyell's book *Principles of Geology* with him on his voyage around the world in the *Beagle*.

Who made the first spring-driven clock?

In the early 1500s a German clockmaker named Peter Heinlein made a clock driven by a spring (instead of by weights). The drawback of early spring clocks was that they ran fastest when the spring was wound tight, and gradually slowed down as the spring became looser.

Who believed that history repeated itself?

The Maya people of Central America were expert astronomers and mathematicians. They believed that time moved in cycles, controlled by gods. A very important cycle was repeated every 52 years.

Who paid for his observatory by selling gunpowder?

In the 1670s King Charles II of England ordered the building of the Greenwich Observatory. However, the first Astronomer Royal, John Flamsteed, had to pay for his own equipment. To raise money, he sold some old (and probably unusable) gunpowder to the French.

Who grouped the stars in constellations?

The ancient Greeks could see some 4,000 stars with the naked eye. They grouped them into constellations. Our word *astronomer* comes from the Greek words meaning "one who arranges stars."

Whose steam carriage service caused a stir?

Sir Goldsworth Gurney built a steam carriage, which in 1831 ran a passenger service between Gloucester and Cheltenham in England. The steam carriage worked well, but people protested along the route and Gurney had to give up his experiment.

Who sailed the oceans in a reed boat to prove a point?

The Norwegian Thor Heyerdahl crossed the Pacific Ocean on a balsa wood raft in 1947, and sailed the Atlantic in a reed boat (called *Ra*) in 1970. He wanted to show that "primitive" craft could make long voyages across rough seas. His voyages also suggested that people might have sailed from America to Polynesia, and from Africa to America, thousands of years ago.

Who made it possible to broadcast sounds by radio?

Marconi pioneered radio *telegraphy*, but radio *telephony* (the sending of speech and music by radio) came a little later. It was made possible by the invention of the thermionic valve (by Ambrose Fleming) and of the improved "triode" or audion valve (by Lee De Forest).

Who invented the barometer?

The first simple barometer was invented in 1643 by Evangelista Torricelli (who had studied under Galileo). It consisted of a glass tube open at one end and filled with mercury. When it was put in a dish of mercury, open-end down, the pressure of the atmosphere forced the mercury in the tube to rise.

Who was the greatest Russian pioneer of spaceflight?

Konstantin Tsiolkovski (1857–1935) was a Russian schoolteacher and scientist. In 1903 (the same year as the Wright brothers' first flight) he worked out that the only way to fly into space was by using a liquid-fueled rocket. His ideas inspired later engineers to build such rockets.

Who used an old garden hose to make a bicycle tire?

John Boyd Dunlop invented the pneumatic (air-filled) tire in the 1880s. His son asked him to improve the solid tires of his tricycle, so Dunlop cut a length of garden hose, stuck the ends together, and pumped it full of air.

Who dug the first river tunnel in the world?

The first tunnel to carry traffic beneath a river was the Thames tunnel linking Rotherhithe and Wapping in London. It was designed by Marc Isambard Brunel. Begun in 1825, the tunnel took 18 years to complete. The river broke into it 11 times. It was the first tunnel to be built with the aid of a tunneling shield (invented by Brunel).

Who built the first radio telescope?

In 1932 the American scientist Karl Jansky was the first to detect radio waves reaching Earth from outer space.

Who caught a cold while carrying out an experiment in food preservation?

Sir Francis Bacon (1561–1626) was a famous English statesman and writer, as well as a scientist. In midwinter he went out to stuff a dead chicken with ice, to see if this would keep the meat fresher. Unfortunately, he caught cold, became ill, and died.

Who invented a water-jet boat?

The first person to suggest using a jet of steam to push a boat along was an American, John Fitch. The first engineer to build a boat driven by water jets was James Ramsey, who tried it out on the Potomac River in Virginia in 1787. It managed a speed of 4 mph.

Who would use a theodolite?

The theodolite is an instrument used by surveyors to measure horizontal and vertical angles.

What is a cyclotron?

The cyclotron, first built by E. O. Lawrence, is a particle accelerator, used to study atomic particles.

WHAT?

What is rayon made of?

Rayon was one of the first artificial textiles. Invented in 1883 (though not made in factories until the early 1900s), it is made from wood pulp containing cellulose.

What is chromatography?

This is a technique used by scientists for separating and analyzing gases, liquids, or substances dissolved in solutions.

What was the Puffing Devil?

In 1801, Richard Trevithick built an iron, steam-powered coach which he called the Puffing Devil. It caused a sensation on its first journey, setting fire to the coach house of an inn.

What is the smallest electrical charge known?

The charge on an electron is the smallest electrical quantity. It was measured by Robert A. Millikan of the US in 1911.

What is quicklime?

Quicklime is made by heating limestone to more than 1,022°F. This gets rid of the carbon dioxide in the limestone, and leaves a white solid—quicklime.

What were limelights?

The stage in old theaters was lit by lights in which calcium was heated until it glowed brilliant white. From this we get the expression "to be in the limelight."

What is the chemical name for vinegar?

Vinegar is a dilute (watered-down) form of acetic acid (also known as ethanoic acid). Vinegar is made by fermenting beer or wine.

What is spectroscopy?

Spectroscopy is the study of light given off by an element. When heated until incandescent (glowing), each element gives off a distinctive pattern of light and color.

What is a quark?

Within the nucleus of the atom are particles even tinier than the neutron and proton. Scientists have discovered two groups of such particles, called leptons and hadrons. Quarks are believed to be even smaller particles that make up the hadrons.

What do microchips look like?

Microchips look like tiny boxes with rows of pins sticking out. The chip inside is made from a thin slice of semiconductor material (usually silicon). Sandwiched inside are layers of even tinier components.

What was the last planet to be discovered?

The last of the nine planets in the solar system to be discovered was Pluto, in 1930. It is so far away from the Sun that it takes 248 Earth-years to make one orbit.

What was an autogyro?

This was a forerunner of the helicopter. It was invented by a Spaniard, Juan de la Cierva, in 1928. The autogyro had wings and a propeller (like an airplane) as well as a rotor (like a helicopter). It could take off and land in a very short distance.

What is the reduction process used for?

Reduction means taking the oxygen out of a substance by heating it. It is used to change oxide mineral ores (such as those of iron and tin) to pure metal.

What is pi?

The Greek letter π, or pi, is used in mathematics for the ratio of the circumference of a circle to its diameter. The value of pi has been worked out to 500,000 decimal places. A useful everyday value for pi is 3.1416.

What is a compound steam engine?

This type of steam engine has two sets of cylinders. Steam passes from a small high-pressure cylinder to a larger low-pressure cylinder. Compounding makes more efficient use of the steam.

What was the world's first iron warship?

The French 36-gun ship *La Gloire*, launched in 1858, was the first warship to be armored with iron plates (although its hull was wooden).

What is incandescence?

When wire is heated until red-hot, it glows with light. This is called incandescence. Often the colors in the light merge, but when a gas becomes incandescent, it will give of a spectrum containing distinctive colors.

What made English villagers run away in 1865?

In 1865 an inventor named Thomas Aveling built the world's first steamroller. He drove it around the lanes of the English village of Kent, and villagers and animals fled in panic at the sight and sound of this puffing, clanking monster.

What is ordinary window glass made from?

The glass used in most windows is soda glass, made from a mixture of lime, soda, and sand.

What do plasticizers do?

These chemicals can change stiff plastics into plastics that can be folded as easily as cloth.

What are the chances of there being other planets like the Earth?

One scientist has calculated that there is a 1 in 2,000 chance of another planet similar to the Earth orbiting a star like our Sun.

What is a dihedral?

In aeronautics, a dihedral is the angle at which an aircraft's wings are tilted up or down.

What was Railroad-Powder?

After Alfred Nobel invented dynamite in 1866, others were quick to try to steal the invention. They used Nobel's formula with tiny changes. Railroad-Powder was an example, marketed in the United States.

What are woofers and tweeters?

These are types of loudspeakers. A woofer has a large diaphragm and works well with low sound frequencies. A tweeter has a smaller diaphragm which responds better to high frequencies.

What are perfect numbers?

A perfect number is one that is equal to the sum of all the numbers that will divide exactly into it. For example, $6 = 1 + 2 + 3$ (and can be divided by 1, 2, and 3). Only 12 perfect numbers are known, and all can be divided exactly by 6.

What is a pulsar?

Pulsars are spinning stars which give off regular pulses of energy, mostly radio waves. They were discovered in 1967.

What was nicknamed the Squirt?

Britain's first jet plane, the Gloster E28/39, first flew in May 1941. Officially called the Pioneer, it became known as the Squirt.

What is corundum?

Corundum, or emery, is a form of aluminum oxide and one of the hardest minerals known. It is used to tip drills, to line furnaces, and as an abrasive.

What is measured in pascals?

The pascal is a unit of pressure in the metric system. It is equal to a force of one newton per square meter. (In the Imperial system, pressure is measured in pounds per square foot.)

What are mineral spirits made from?

The mineral spirits sold to clean paintbrushes are a mixture of hydrocarbons and are made from petroleum.

What is the science of geodesy?

Geodesy is the branch of science which studies the shape and size of the Earth and the strength of gravity over its surface. It tries to position points on the Earth's surface by measuring the lengths and directions of lines, making allowance for the planet's curved shape.

What does a pitot tube measure?

This is a device for measuring the speed of a fluid. Pitot tubes are used to measure the speed of a river's flow and the air speed of aircraft. They are named after their inventor, Henri Pitot (1695–1771).

What is fool's gold?

Iron pyrites, a mineral form of iron sulfide, looks like gold but is much harder. Prospectors often mistook this "fool's gold" for the real thing.

What is earthshine?

Earthshine is sunlight reflected from the Earth. An astronaut in space may see a spacecraft lit by earthlight (as we see Moon light on a clear night).

What is the Appleton layer?

This is a layer in the ionosphere, also known as the F layer. It reflects radio waves and is named after Sir Edward Appleton (1892–1965).

What is the Fata Morgana?

A famous mirage, seen in the Straits of Messina, off southern Italy. People on land see ships and buildings (sometimes both right way up and upside down) on the sea or in the air. The strange effects are caused by the bending of light rays passing through warm air.

What were "cat whiskers"?

In the early days of radio broadcasting in the 1920s, people listened on headphones. Inside the simple radio sets were crystal detectors with very thin wires, which had to be constantly adjusted. The wires were known as cat whiskers.

What is the seafloor like?

At the bottom of the ocean lies the abyssal plain, at an average depth of 2.5 miles. It is covered with slimy ooze, the remains of dead animals, and plants that sank down from the waters above.

What is the Humboldt current?

The Humboldt current is a cold ocean current which flows north up the west coast of South America. It carries cold water from the Antarctic as far north as the equator and is named after its discoverer, Alexander von Humboldt (1769–1859).

What is made by the Haber process?

The Haber process is used in industry to make ammonia by a reaction of nitrogen with hydrogen. Quantities of ammonia are used in making fertilizers, explosives, and dyes.

What does a flywheel do?

Steam and gasoline engines both have flywheels. These heavy wheels are placed between the pistons and drive shaft. They spin easily to "smooth out" the jerky effect of the pistons' movement.

What are carbon fibers?

Carbon fibers are made by heating acrylic fibers until they become pure carbon. The fine threads are mixed with plastic to make a light but strong material used for car and aircraft parts and tennis racquets.

What was a noria?

This ancient machine was used to raise water. An undershot waterwheel was turned by a running stream. Buckets attached to the rim of the wheel were filled, raised to the top, and then emptied into an irrigation ditch.

What was the cosmic engine?

In 1092 the Chinese inventor Su Sung built a clock driven by a waterwheel. It turned other wheels to make bells ring, gongs sound, and figures appear holding signs to tell the hours. The "cosmic engine" ran for 30 years.

WHERE?

Where was the first photograph taken?

The earliest photograph still in existence was taken from a window in Gras, France, in 1826 by Joseph Niépce. It was fixed on a pewter plate.

Where would you find isotherms and isobars?

On a map or weather chart. Isotherms are lines joining places where the temperature is the same. Isobars are lines joining places where the air pressure is the same.

Where might a person experience a "whiteout"?

In snowy regions, the snow reflects sunlight. Where this reflected light is the same as the light reflected from clouds, the horizon may disappear. Land and sky merge into one and a traveler may become confused.

Where is the world's biggest radio telescope?

The largest radio telescope is at Arecibo, Puerto Rico. It is 1,000 yards across and was built inside a natural crater. Its disadvantage over smaller instruments is that it cannot be steered to line up on a particular radio source.

Where is the Ring of Fire?

This name is given to an area around the Pacific Ocean where earthquakes and volcanoes are common.

Where was the world's worst earthquake?

The earthquake which caused most loss of life struck the Tangshan region of China in 1976. It is believed that 750,000 people died.

Where did the world's largest raindrop fall?

The world's biggest raindrop was measured over Hawaii in 1979. It was 0.3 inches in diameter.

Where was gas street lighting first used?

A Scot named William Murdock experimented in the 1790s with gas lamps in his home and in a Birmingham factory. The first London street to have gas lamps was Pall Mall in 1807.

Where are Bunsen burners used?

Bunsen burners are small gas jets used in scientific laboratories. The amount of air (and therefore the type of flame) is controlled by moving a sleeve on the burner's tube. The burner is named after the German chemist Robert Bunsen (1811–99).

Where was the world's first nuclear power station?

A Soviet power station started working in 1954. But the first nuclear plant to generate electricity for domestic use was Calder Hall in Britain, which was opened in 1956.

Where is the radius of a circle?

The radius of a circle is a straight line from the center to the edge. To find the area of a circle, use the formula:
Area $= \pi r^2$ ($\pi =$ pi $= 3.1416$; r $=$ radius).

Where are synchronous satellites found?

If a satellite orbits the Earth at a distance of 22,245 miles, it will remain "stationary" above the same spot on the Earth's surface. The first such satellite was launched in 1963. Synchronous satellites are used for communications.

Where did the first tank enter battle?

During the Battle of the Somme in World War I, a new weapon made its first appearance. This was the tank. It was first seen in action in September 1916 when a single machine with a crew of eight crawled toward the German trenches.

Where did the Wright brothers make their first flight?

The Wrights launched their first airplane, *Flyer 1*, from a sand mound (known as Kill Devil Hill) at Kitty Hawk in North Carolina, in 1903.

Where did Edison sell newspapers?

At the age of 12, the famous inventor Thomas Alva Edison sold newspapers on board a railroad train traveling each day to Detroit, Michigan. He set up a laboratory on board so that he could carry out experiments while the train waited to make the return trip in the evening.

Where is the world's largest active volcano?

Mauna Loa in Hawaii erupts about every three and a half years. Its height above sea level is 13,680 feet but even more of the giant volcano is below sea level.

Where is the world's largest desert?

The Sahara is the biggest desert on Earth. Its area is roughly 3.2 million square miles.

Where was the world's greatest known natural explosion?

In 1883 the island volcano of Krakatoa, south of Sumatra, exploded. The third and largest bang was heard almost 3,000 miles away. Dust and rock from the explosion were carried all around the world in the atmosphere.

Where was the world's first hotel elevator built?

A hotel in New York boasted the first elevator in 1859. It worked on a screw system. The first office-building elevator came in 1868.

Where did people eat a frozen-food banquet in 1873?

James Harrison, whose ice-making techniques helped establish the refrigerated meat trade between Australia and England, held this unusual feast in Melbourne, Australia. He served meat, chicken, and fish which had been kept in a deep freeze for six months.

Where are an aircraft's elevators?

Elevators are hinged horizontal planes on the tail of an aircraft. When the elevators are lowered, the tail is pushed up and the aircraft dives.

Where is Britain's oldest clock?

The oldest clock in Britain is in Salisbury Cathedral in Wiltshire, England. It was made around 1386 and was working until the late 1800s.

Where would you find a canard wing?

Some high-speed aircraft have small, extra wings at the front of the fuselage. This design is known as a canard wing.

Where were bouncing bombs used to bust dams?

During World War II British bombers breached reservoir dams in Germany with bouncing bombs. The bombs' designer, Barnes Wallis, got the idea from skimming stones across water. The bombers dropped each bomb at a precise height so that it skipped across the water of the reservoir, hit the dam wall, and then sank before exploding.

Where was the first modern lighthouse?

Modern lighthouses are based on the design of John Smeaton, who built a lighthouse on the Eddystone Rock off Plymouth, England, in 1759. It was the third lighthouse on the rock and lasted until 1882.

Where were knotted ropes used for measuring?

The Egyptians used knotted ropes to work out problems in geometry.

Where do most meteorites fall?

Since more than 71 percent of the Earth is covered by ocean, most meteorites fall into the sea and so can never be studied. Nearly 2,000 meteorites have been recorded as hitting the land since the early 1600s.

Where is the world's largest optical telescope?

The largest optical telescope is the 236-inch reflector at the Caucasus observatory in the USSR. It was completed in 1976. The largest in the US is the 200-inch Hale telescope at Mount Palomar, California.

WHEN?

When did an eclipse stop a battle?

An eclipse of the Sun is a dramatic happening. In 585 B.C. an eclipse stopped a battle between the armies of Lydia and Media (in Asia Minor). Both sides were so frightened by the sudden darkness that they fled.

When were the first snapshots taken?

Photography caught on with the public after 1888, when the first Kodak box cameras (using celluloid roll film) went on sale. They were cheap and simple to use.

When was steam printing machinery first used?

All books and newspapers were printed by hand, one sheet at a time, until the early 1800s. A German printer named Friedrich König invented a mechanical press able to print 1,200 sheets an hour.

When was the first gas turbine car built?

Gas turbine cars were tested after World War II. The first one was built in Britain by Rover in 1950.

When was the first manned spaceflight?

On April 12, 1961, a Soviet Vostok spacecraft was launched. On board was cosmonaut Yuri Gagarin, who made an historic one-orbit flight around the Earth.

When was prestressed concrete invented?

Prestressed concrete is made by inserting stretched steel wires into wet concrete, and keeping the wires stretched until the concrete sets. It was developed in the 1930s, particularly for long single-span bridges.

When was the photocopier invented?

The photocopier was invented by an American, Chester Carlson, in 1940.

When was the first public address system used?

In 1916 the Bell Telephone Company set up an open-air electric loudspeaker system at Staten Island, New York. This was the first modern public address system; until then simple megaphones had been used to help a speaker's voice carry farther.

When was phosgene used as a weapon?

Phosgene is a colorless gas that smells like new-mown hay. Its chemical name is carbonyl chloride. It is poisonous and was used against troops during World War I (1914–1918), when chemical weapons made their first appearance on the battlefield.

When will Halley's comet return?

Halley's comet has an orbit around the Sun that brings it close to Earth every 75-76 years. Since Edmund Halley saw it in 1682, it has returned in 1758, 1835, 1910, and 1986. It should be back again in 2062.

When was algebra invented?

Algebra (using letters to represent mathematical quantities) was developed after geometry. It seems to have been used in ancient Egypt, Babylonia, China, and India. The name comes from the Arabic *al-jabr*. The symbols we use (such as x and y) were not common until after the 1600s.

When were fingerprints first taken to catch criminals?

A system for taking and comparing fingerprints was developed in Britain by Sir Edward Henry and adopted by Scotland Yard in 1901.

When did the first step rocket fly?

A step, or multistage, rocket was an essential first step toward the conquest of space. In 1949 the Americans tested a German V2 with a smaller WAC Corporal rocket on top. At a height of 20 miles the Corporal separated from the V2 booster and fired its own engine which accelerated it to a speed of nearly 5,600 mph and a height of 250 miles.

When were the first Nobel prizes awarded?

Alfred Nobel, inventor of dynamite, died in 1896. He had become very wealthy and wanted to use his wealth to endow prizes for achievement in physics, chemistry, medicine, literature, and the promotion of peace. The Nobel Foundation was set up and the first prizes were awarded in 1901. (A sixth prize, for economics, was later added.)

When did father and son share a Nobel prize?

In 1915 the British scientists William Henry Bragg and his son William Lawrence Bragg shared the Nobel prize for physics for their work on X-rays and crystals.

When was the Hovercraft invented?

The Hovercraft was the invention of Christopher Cockerell of Britain (1955). The first practical craft, the SRN-1, made its first trip in 1959.

When did steam turbines first power a battleship?

The British battleship *Dreadnought* (1906) was the first of a new class of super-warships. Faster and more heavily armored than any of its rivals, *Dreadnought* was the first battleship to have steam turbine engines.

When will the world run out of minerals?

At the rate we are currently using up existing supplies, silver, zinc, and mercury will be exhausted in 25 years. Tin and copper reserves will last roughly 40 years. Iron and aluminum will be used up in 60 years.

When were 3-D films first shown?

In the 1950s (and in an attempt to lure people away from television and back into the theaters) 3-D films were shown. They were made with a twin-lens camera which produced two images projected onto the screen. The audience had to wear glasses with differently polarized lenses (so that each eye saw only one image). Nobody liked wearing them and so 3-D films did not catch on.

When was nylon first made?

Nylon was invented in 1935 by the American chemist Wallace H. Carothers, working for the Du Pont laboratories. Nylon stockings went on sale that same year.

When did people first make pots on a wheel?

The potter's wheel was one of the earliest human inventions. People in the Middle East and Asia Minor were turning clay pots on wheels more than 8,500 years ago.

When did a steam-engined airship fly?

In 1852 Henri Giffard of France built a cigar-shaped steerable airship. It had a propeller turned by a steam engine. Giffard's design was ahead of its time, but a lighter, safer engine was needed to make airships a success.

When were navigation buoys first used?

Buoys to guide ships in and out of a harbor, and away from dangerous rocks, were used in Europe as early as the 1100s. Modern buoys have lights, radar beacons, and electronic aids to guide shipping.

When was the bicycle chain invented?

The flexible cycle chain was invented by Hans Renold, a Swiss working in England, in the 1880s.

When did people first have electric heaters?

Electric "lamp radiators" went on sale in 1896. They had large bulbs which radiated heat. In 1912 the Belling heating element (a wire wound around a fired clay tube) appeared.

When were cars banned from traveling at more than walking speed?

Until it was abolished in 1896, a British law banned any "horseless carriage" from traveling on public roads at more than 4 mph. Higher speeds, it was feared, would endanger other road users, particularly horses.

WHY?

Why do things burn?

Burning, or combustion, is a chemical reaction between a substance and the oxygen in the air. Heat is given off and a flame may be seen. Burning cannot happen without oxygen.

Why do some street lights glow orange-yellow?

The color in orange-yellow street lights comes from the sodium vapor inside. The yellowish color is characteristic of all sodium compounds.

Why do water pipes burst in cold weather?

When water freezes, it expands. This is why a pipe filled with water may be cracked when the liquid turns to ice in very cold weather.

Why does humus make soil more fertile?

Humus enriches the topsoil in which plants grow. It is made by bacteria in the soil which break down, or rot, vegetation. To do this most effectively, bacteria need warmth, air, and plenty of plant matter to work on. This is why gardeners put rubbish on a compost heap. In a few weeks, the rubbish is broken down into good, rich humus.

Why can a sand dune move across a desert?

Sand dunes, like waves in the ocean, are moved by the wind. The tiny sand grains are blown up the gentle windward slope, and then roll down the steeper leeward side. The whole dune advances in this manner.

Why do the stars twinkle?

To an astronaut in space, the stars do not twinkle. The twinkling is caused by the starlight passing through the Earth's atmosphere. The hot and cold layers of air cause the light to flicker.

Why did some Russians spend a year in bed?

To help research into the medical effects on astronauts of long spaceflights, Russian volunteers spent a year in bed. They lay with their heads 6 inches lower than their feet, to simulate the effects of prolonged weightlessness, and were given drugs to test the effects on their bodies and mental health. One volunteer grew nearly 2 inches taller!

Why is Portland cement so named?

In 1824 Joseph Aspdin invented a cement made from clay and limestone. He called it Portland cement, after the gray Portland stone used to construct many buildings in London at the time.

Why was Nikola Tesla a great scientist?

Tesla was born in what is now Yugoslavia in 1856. He emigrated to the US and worked for a time with Thomas Edison. Tesla developed an electrical power system based on alternating current (AC), which is better than direct current (DC) for transmission over long distance. It was eventually adopted in America.

Why do epoxy adhesives come in two tubes?

Many commercial adhesives are sold in two-tube packs. One tube contains the adhesive epoxide, the other a chemical catalyst that sets off the reaction to make the adhesive stick. The two must be mixed in the right proportions to make the adhesive harden. Once hard, the adhesive cannot be softened.

Why could horses not pull apart two copper bowls?

In 1654 the German scientist Otto von Guericke demonstrated the amazing power of the vacuum. He placed two copper bowls together to form a sphere, and pumped out all the air inside. He then had horses harnessed to each bowl and challenged his audience. Could the horses pull the two bowls apart? Strain as they might, the horses failed, because the vacuum sphere was held tightly together by the pressure of the air all around it.

Why do oil and water not mix?

Oil and water are said to be *immiscible*; they do not form a solution. If stirred, they form a mixture of droplets which soon separates into two layers with the oil on top.

Why does a car's antifreeze work?

In cold weather, the water in a car's cooling system may freeze. Antifreeze contains a chemical such as ethylene glycol with a low freezing point. This makes it unlikely that the cooling system will freeze in winter.

Why does nondrip paint not drip?

Nondrip paints are *colloids* – suspensions of substances, halfway between mixtures and solutions. The colloids used in nondrip paints are known as gels. They are normally jellylike (and so don't drip). But when stirred or brushed, they liquefy and spread easily.

Why does syrup flow slowly?

Syrup has high viscosity. In other words, it is slowed down easily as it moves. Water has low viscosity and flows quickly.

Why must white phosphorus be stored under water?

White phosphorus glows in the dark and catches fire as soon as it is exposed to the air. It must therefore always be stored under water.

Why does a compact disc last longer than a plastic record?

Plastic records are worn as the stylus travels around the playing grooves. The laser beam in a compact disc player does not touch the surface of the disc in order to produce sound. Therefore the disc lasts much longer.

Why does mercury have the chemical symbol Hg?

Mercury was originally given the name Hydrargyrus, meaning "liquid silver" in Latin. From this old name comes its modern symbol, Hg.

Why have electric cars not yet been mass produced?

Electric cars are quiet, cheap, and do not pollute the air. However, they depend for their power on batteries and these must be recharged regularly. No battery yet made lasts long enough to make the electric car a rival to the gasoline-driven vehicle.

Why is yellow a warning color for scientists?

Although red is a common "danger" color, inside a laboratory warning signs are usually in yellow (which is more easily seen).

Why were Greek temples made up of straight lines?

The ancient Greeks did not use the arch. Their buildings had vertical walls, with roof beams laid across from side to side. For this reason, no Greek building could be very wide unless rows of pillars were inserted to support the roof.

Why doesn't a ladder fall over?

A ladder leaning at the correct angle against a wall is balanced, or "in equilibrium." The weight of the ladder, and of the person on it, is balanced by reaction to the weight and friction at each end of the ladder. If too much weight is put on the ladder, the equilibrium can be upset.

Why are nickel-cadmium batteries useful?

Nickel-cadmium batteries are small enough to be used in an electric razor and they can be recharged (like an accumulator, or car battery, which is much bigger).

Why did early computers use punched cards?

The information a computer needs is provided as numbers in binary code. In the first computers, this was done by feeding in cards on which holes had been punched. The coded holes formed pulses of electricity which were fed to the electronic circuits in the computer.

HOW?

How can frost crack rocks?

When water freezes to ice, it expands. Rainwater collecting in a cracked rock will expand when frozen, and the ice pressing against the crack can split off a piece.

How do atoms join together?

Atoms join together to form molecules in *bonds*. Sometimes they share electrons (in a *covalent* bond), each atom giving one electron to make the bond. Another kind of bond is called an *electrovalent* bond.

How much space "junk" is orbiting the Earth?

There are about 7,000 items of junk in space. They include old satellites, bits of booster rocket, and even a screwdriver lost by an astronaut.

How can farm manure be used as fuel?

Animal dung ferments when stored inside a sunken tank. As it ferments, it gives off methane gas, and this gas can be piped off and burned as heating fuel.

How fast was the fastest ocean liner?

The last holder of the Blue Riband for a transatlantic crossing by a passenger liner was the US liner *United States*. In 1952 it crossed the Atlantic in 3 days, 12 hours, and 12 minutes. Its top speed was almost 42 knots (48 mph).

How thick are Saturn's rings?

Saturn's rings are some 168,000 miles across, but only 5 miles thick. They are made of ice, dust, and large boulders.

How many moving parts are there in a car engine?

Most car engines have around 200 moving parts.

How is wrought iron made?

Wrought iron is made by remelting pig iron with iron ore. The mixture is then hammered or pressed to make a form of iron that is tougher and more resistant to corrosion than ordinary iron.

How does an ornithopter fly?

An ornithopter is an aircraft with flapping wings. A model ornithopter, made of the lightest materials and powered by a rubber band, will fly well inside a large room.

How do you work out the area of a triangle?

To find the area of a triangle, first measure the base and height. Then multiply the two dimensions, and divide by two.

How many planets in the solar system have rings?

Saturn was thought to be the only planet with rings until the 1970s when Jupiter and Uranus were also found to have rings.

How were the first canned foods tested?

In the early 1800s canned foods were tested by being stored in a hot room for a month. If the tin exploded, the contents were obviously bad. If not, all was well.

How many sorts of rocks are there?

All rocks belong to three main groups, depending on how they were formed. These groups are *sedimentary* rocks, *igneous* rocks, and *metamorphic* rocks.

How long is a Myr?

Scientists use the Myr to measure geological time. One Myr = 1 million years ago. The Earth was "born" in 4500 Myr.

How hard is a coin?

A bronze coin is about 3 in the Mohs scale: softer than glass but harder than a fingernail.

How did the last Apollo astronauts explore the Moon?

Apollos 15, 16, and *17* were the last missions in the series of American Moon landings (1969–72). The astronauts rode around in wheeled vehicles, known as lunar rovers, and were able to venture much farther afield than the first lunar astronauts who explored on foot.

How is glass made ovenproof?

Ovenproof glass is made by adding boron oxide instead of silicon to the mixture. This makes it tougher and better able to resist temperature changes.

How high are the highest clouds?

Cirrus clouds are found at a height of up to 8.7 miles. But the rare nacreous (mother of pearl) clouds sometimes form much higher still, at around 16 miles.

How many faces does a dodecahedron have?

A dodecahedron is a regular solid with 12 faces. Garnet is an example of a mineral crystal which is a dodecahedron.

How fast is the population growing?

Twenty thousand years ago, there were fewer than five million people on Earth. Two thousand years ago, there were 200 million. Two hundred years ago, there were 900 million. Today, there are more than 5,000 million.

How much bigger than the Earth is the Sun?

The Sun has a diameter more than 100 times greater than that of the Earth. The Sun's material is less dense than the Earth's, but even so it has a mass 330,000 times as great.

How does a thermocouple work?

A thermocouple makes electricity from heat. If two unlike metals are joined together in a circuit, and then warmed, a current will flow in the circuit.

How hot is it on the planet nearest the Sun?

Mercury is the planet nearest to the Sun. The temperature on Mercury is about 932°F, hot enough to melt lead. The Sun itself is roughly 11 times hotter!

How big are shooting stars?

Shooting stars, or meteorites, are mostly very small. Some are no larger than a grain of sand. Thousands burn up in the Earth's atmosphere every day.

How long must a pendulum be?

To make it swing once every second at the equator, a pendulum must be 39 inches long. But in higher latitudes, it must be longer. To swing once a second in London, a pendulum must be 39.11 inches long. The difference is caused by difference in the Earth's gravitational pull.

How far can a nuclear submarine travel without refueling?

In 1960 the USS *Triton* sailed around the world underwater (a distance of 42,000 miles) in three months without refueling. Its fuel was a charge of uranium the size of an electric light bulb.

How hot is an acetylene torch?

When acetylene (also known as ethyne) burns in oxygen it produces a very hot flame – with a temperature of about 5,400°F. This heat is put to use in the acetylene welding torch.

How did oxygen get its name?

The word *oxygen* means "acid making." Oxygen was given this name by the French scientist Antoine Lavoisier who thought that all acids contained oxygen. He was wrong, but the name has stuck.

How many degrees are there in a triangle?

No matter what its shape, the angles of any triangle always add up to 180 degrees.

Index

INDEX

PHOTOGRAPHIC ACKNOWLEDGMENTS

The publishers would like to thank the following for kindly supplying photographs for this book:

Page 8 The Mansell Collection; 9 Cavendish Laboratory, Cambridge; 11 Novosti Press Agency; 12 Frank Spooner Pictures; 14 ZEFA; 18 Science Photo Library; 25 ZEFA *top*, Michael Holford *right*, ZEFA *bottom*; 26 ZEFA; 27 Science Photo Library; 28 BOC Ltd *left*, ZEFA *right*; 30 The Mansell Collection *top*, Robin Kerrod *bottom*; 32 Science Photo Library; 33 Central Electricity Generating Board; 34 The Mansell Collection; 36 The Science Museum, London; 37 Neil Lorimer; 38 RLP Ltd; 40 NASA; 42 INTEL Corp *left*, IBM *right*; 43 Cray Research Inc; 45 The Kobal Collection *top*, ZEFA *bottom*; 46 Nature Photographers; 47 Holt Studios Ltd; 51 J. Allen Cash; 52 ZEFA; 53 Science Photo Library; 54 The Science Museum, London; 56 Kodak Ltd *left*, ZEFA *right*; 57 G.R.E.; 58 Science Photo Library; 59 WHO Group; 60 Paul Brierly *top*, ZEFA *bottom*; 61 Science Photo Library; 62 University College Hospital; 65 Shell Photographic Library *left*, ZEFA *right*; 71 ZEFA; 73 Supersport; 74 All-sport; 75 NASA; 78 Mary Evans Picture Library; 79 Giraudon; 83 ZEFA; 84 The Science Museum, London; 85 Ronan Picture Library *left*, Hulton Picture Library *right*; 87 ZEFA; 90 Science Photo Library; 95 New Zealand House; 96 ZEFA; 98 ZEFA; 102 Frank Lane Picture Agency; 103 ZEFA; 108 Popperfoto; 111 Iron Bridge Museum; 112 Science Photo Library; 114 Tin Research Institute; 119 American Electric Power; 121 Sonia Halliday; 125 ZEFA; 128 Haymarket Publishing; 129 Popperfoto; 131 Mary Evan Picture Library; 134 The Mansell Collection; 135 Mary Evans Picture Library; 137 NASA; 139 Mary Evans Picture Library; 140 Mary Evans Picture Library; 141 The Kobal Collection.

Picture Research: Sarah Donald and Elaine Willis